MILITARY MILLIONAIRES

THIRD EDITION

Personal financial stories shared by members of the US military and definitions of modern investment tools.

MICHAEL STEPHEN HAMLIN

Copyright © 2013 by Michael S. Hamlin

ISBN: 978-0-692-02028-9

Library of Congress Control Number: 2013945707

All Rights Reserved. No part of this book may be reproduced or transmitted in any form or by any means, electronic or mechanical, including photocopying, recording, or by any information storage and retrieval system without written permission from the author, except for the inclusion of brief quotations in a review.

Printed in the United States of America.

This book has been dedicated to all military veterans of the United States of America.

Thank you for your service.

Contents

Chapter 1	Your Very First Paycheck	1
Chapter 2	Take Advantage of Your Advantages	5
Chapter 3	Why Is Time So Important?	13
Chapter 4	Straight from the Top	22
Chapter 5	Why Are Financial Investments So Mysterious?	28
Chapter 6	Continue to Educate Yourself.	34
Chapter 7	Basic Training.	36
Chapter 8	Self-Made Millionaire	43
Chapter 9	How Do You Envision Your Lifestyle During Retirement?	46
Chapter 10	Off to a Great Start	55
Chapter 11	Making a Tentative Plan	58
Chapter 12	Budget Examples.	65

CHAPTER 13	A Shared Vision	73
CHAPTER 14	Needs Versus Wants	75
CHAPTER 15	Simple Can Be Effective	85
CHAPTER 16	Where Do I Begin Investing?	87
CHAPTER 17	Conquering a Mountain	97
CHAPTER 18	Eliminating Debt…It's an Uphill Battle	99
CHAPTER 19	Start Small and Grow Big	110
CHAPTER 20	Types of Investments	113
CHAPTER 21	How Much Should I Invest?	125
CHAPTER 22	Personal Finance Readjustment	131
CHAPTER 23	Choosing a Financial Planner	134
CHAPTER 24	Day Trader	140
CHAPTER 25	Deployment Finance	144
CHAPTER 26	Money Saving Tips	158
CHAPTER 27	A Final Success Story	168
CHAPTER 28	Summary	171

INTRODUCTION

Who should read this book? Every military service member. Why should you read this book? To learn how to accumulate wealth and the advantages of doing so while serving in the military. When should you read this book? Today!

My intent is to educate you, the military service member, about the enormous advantages that can be gained by establishing a financial savings plan early in your career while determining how to strike a balance between responsible spending and the peace of mind that a financial savings plan can offer.

As a serviceman or -woman in the US military, you can use this book to explore your economic potential. If you want to learn how to create your own long-term financial plan while avoiding the numerous pitfalls along the way, this book is for you.

As a service member, you have the ability to accumulate a substantial amount of money for your retirement in addition to your military pension or civilian retirement plan.

Serving in the US military, especially at an early age, can be the financial opportunity of a lifetime. By learning how to handle your finances at the beginning stages of your career, it is highly possible to ensure a secure financial future in less time and with less effort than the average civilian citizen.

Imagine: in addition to serving proudly in the United States military, you also have the capability to position yourself to retire earlier than the average civilian. As you continue reading, a clear picture will emerge of how making conservative monetary adjustments to your lifestyle now can substantially impact your personal finances in the future.

I wrote this book in an effort to promote financial prosperity among service members from every branch of the United States military who have unselfishly devoted their lives to serving our great nation. Applying this vital information early in your military career will allow you to stabilize your finances and promote a significant quality of life for both yourself and your family.

This book is intended to be used as an educational reference only, and by no means does the author intend to advise on specific investments for your plan or how you invest your hard-earned military pay. Use the book to educate yourself about the time-proven investment tools, techniques, theories, and strategies. You must then decide what financial plan works best for you. My methods of teaching you include definitions of financial terms, mathematical demonstrations of financial concepts, and anecdotal stories of fictionalized military members.

The anecdotes are based on my observations during four years of military service and on my imagination of illustrations concerning the right and wrong ways to obtain financial security. Any resemblance of anecdotal characters to real persons, names, or ranks are coincidental and not intended to portray actual persons; except chapter 27 does parallel the story of an actual military person who gave permission to use the information.

In the military we learn our jobs during basic training and advanced training by methods that include repetition. The information you need to insure financial security is repeated in different ways throughout this book. My expectation is that you will become clear about the concepts and convinced of their validity as you read the book from beginning to end.

All financial examples use simple arithmetic and do not consider fluctuating markets, taxes or other life factors that could significantly reduce numerical gains in the illustrations given. All examples are exactly that: examples. They are used only to emphasize the importance of investing as early as possible. It is imperative to remember that a market's past performance does not guarantee future returns.

The author may update *Military Millionaires* with new investment tools, laws, and strategies. However, the information contained within can change without notice due to legislation regarding investing, taxes, military investment options, etc. The author does not claim professional financial expertise regarding specific investments. It is the author's opinion that a novice investor should seek professional financial advice prior to making any investment to ensure that he or she is making fully informed decisions as well as complying with current tax laws and other pertinent statutes.

The concepts in this book are simple; begin saving early; reduce debt quickly; increase amounts placed in savings from time to time, invest wisely; and, most importantly, take advantage of the unique financial opportunities offered by the military service. The various restatements of the concepts together with the definitions, mathematical demonstration, and anecdotes will sharpen your understanding and strengthen your belief that you in fact can attain financial security and build your wealth.

Chapter 1

Your Very First Paycheck

"I've got plenty of time to save money—I'm buying a new car today!"

Private Erickson
US Army

A brand new car. That's exactly what I should do. Buy myself a brand new car. Why shouldn't I? I just joined the United States military and I deserve a gift. I even saw a television commercial for a dealership that finances 100% for active-duty military. Better yet, I'll use my enlistment bonus and cash I saved during basic training as a down payment. What a great idea.

This was the discussion taking place between eighteen-year-old Private Erickson and me. We'd both enlisted in the US Army and met during our basic training. This was the first

Saturday at our initial duty station. I was in uniform, assigned to Charge of Quarters (CQ), and posted to the front desk of our barracks. Private Erickson was off duty and quoting the fast-talking salesman from the car dealer television commercial.

"What? Hold on a minute. Think about what you're doing," I said.

"No way. I'm going to the dealership right now." And that's exactly what PVT Erickson did.

That evening, still on CQ duty, I received a phone call. It was Private Erickson calling from outside our barracks. Looking out the window, I saw him waving from a brand new luxury SUV and calling from his stylish new cell phone.

"That must have cost forty grand. How are you going to pay for it?" I asked.

"A bank gave me a loan for only $741.03 a month over the next six years. How cool is that?"

"That's ridiculous. How cool will you be when it's necessary to ask the bank for gas money?" I replied.

Erickson sat quietly with a puzzled look of embarrassment.

Although I wanted to explain that the vehicle had already depreciated in value and he now owed more than it was worth, I held back. It was apparent Erickson was beginning to realize his purchases may not have been such wise investments after all.

WHO IS RESPONSIBLE FOR PRIVATE ERICKSON'S FINANCIAL DILEMMA?

In the first week of his military enlistment, Private Erickson had financed a new luxury vehicle for six years and was locked into a costly cell phone contract for three. Unfortunately, similar scenarios occur all too often with people in military service. Uninformed decisions and the powerful enticement of today's luxuries and conveniences undoubtedly affect our judgment. Even worse, it is now commonplace for transactions such as new vehicles to be completed with 100% financing, no cash down.

Yes, Private Erickson made the final decision to live beyond his means. But in order to complete the $40,000 transaction, it took an unscrupulous salesperson as well as a lending institution with liberal guidelines that was willing to accept the questionable risk without considering Private Erickson's well-being. Ultimately, the only person who stood to feel a negative impact was Private Erickson, leaving the others who contributed to his predicament unaffected.

AS YOU CONTINUE READING...

...you will see that I have included a number of stories regarding different financial scenarios. Whether the examples illustrate success or failure, studying them is an excellent way for you to learn effective money-handling concepts.

The stories may:

- Relate to similar financial experiences you have already experienced
- Inspire you to create a financial plan of your own
- Help you overcome financial complications you are currently experiencing

- Ensure that you have the tools necessary to avoid making disastrous money-handling mistakes

From these stories, you will study what other people in similar situations have done under various circumstances. Learning other people's successes and failures may empower you to make the right choices for yourself.

So what exactly is the purpose of this book? It will:

- Help you eliminate the mystery of the unknown in terms of your financial future
- Aid you in making informed financial decisions
- Help you overcome financial obstacles you may be facing right now
- Help you avoid financial pitfalls in the future
- Inspire you to keep moving toward your financial goals
- Assist you in exploring your potential financial prosperity
- Help you ensure a sustainable quality of life

In short, after reading this book, you will be able to attain financial goals you may have never thought possible.

Chapter 2

Take Advantage of Your Advantages

A STEADY INCOME AT A YOUNG AGE

One of the remarkable benefits for recruits entering the military at an early age is the steady source of income immediately received. All young recruits should be aware of this distinct advantage. In addition to the pride you feel with military service, your steady source of income is the opportunity of a lifetime. By contributing to a financial plan from the very start of your enlistment, you can position yourself for significant financial gains.

Based merely on the military pay scale, it may appear that service members do not make a lot of money. The fact of the matter is quite the opposite. When considering the expenses absorbed by benefits received, a sizable portion of a service member's income remains that could potentially be invested for the future.

This is due in large part to the service members' limited financial obligations. In addition to base pay, service members typically have housing and food provided. Civilian college graduates may not begin a savings plan until years later after earning a bachelor's degree or higher. On the other hand, military recruits can begin saving the same amount of money as their civilian counterparts at a significantly earlier age. This seemingly small difference in time can create a tremendous difference in an investment portfolio due to compounding. We'll explore the power of compounding in greater detail in chapter 3.

SERVICE MEMBER VS. COLLEGE GRADUATE

Studies conducted in 2011 show that the average college student owes between $15,000 and $25,000 in loans. Students generally graduate with the requirement of repaying these loans through monthly installments that can stretch over a decade or more. The same amount of money used to repay the student loans would have enormous growth potential if placed in an investment plan instead of being used to meet the minimum monthly installments. Money that is committed to paying a student loan will never reach a graduate's savings account.

Let's take a look at the investment potential between a twenty-five-year-old college graduate and an eighteen-year-old private in the US military. In our scenario, both share a goal of retiring at the age of sixty.

	Years to Age 60	Interest Rate	Monthly Investment	Initial Investment	Accumulated Savings
Student (At College Graduation)	35	4%	$400.00	$0.00	$386,613.13
Recruit who does not invest enlistment bonus	42	4%	$400.00	$0.00	$548,184.79
Recruit who invests enlistment bonus	42	4%	$400.00	$20,000.00 (enlistment bonus)	$627,115.11

As you can see, if the recruit were to include a $20,000 enlistment bonus, there is a difference of nearly a quarter of a million dollars with just seven additional years of saving.

New recruits have decades of potential accumulation and compounding ahead of them. It is easy to earmark a portion of your earnings to be automatically invested in a tax-advantaged retirement account. The benefit of initiating your plan as soon as you've received your first paycheck is the most important lesson in this book.

RETIREMENT: MILITARY VS. CIVILIAN

Completing a twenty- to thirty-year career in the US military gives the service member the opportunity to design a financial plan that potentially could surpass that of the average civilian.

Throughout the course of a working career, civilians often face the challenging task of maintaining retirement funds entirely on their own. Contributions from their employers might improve their bottom lines, but a large portion of their savings will come out of their own pockets. The US military pension, in conjunction with the potential to accumulate a hefty amount of cash in savings, is difficult to match in the private sector, and civilians are not often able to duplicate such a sound retirement package, which includes a health plan.

MONEY-SAVING ADVANTAGES OF SERVING IN THE MILITARY

Let's take a look at some common advantages of serving in the military that are often overlooked.

ON-POST HOUSING AND BARRACKS ACCOMMODATIONS

Quite commonly, the largest monthly expense for a civilian can be a mortgage payment or rent. In the military, you are assigned to a barracks room or officer quarters, where most often your only responsibility is to keep it clean. Married couples may also be able to live in on-post government housing.

There are a number of benefits associated with living in on-post housing:

- Introduction of junior personnel into the military culture
- Promotion of military values

- A sense of community
- Support from neighbors during deployments
- Security
- Convenience (short commute, or no commute at all)
- Cohesiveness with other military families

Although service members and their families consider these nontangible benefits significant, they may not regard them as the deciding factor when determining whether to live on or off post. Primarily, service members choose to live on post for economic reasons, as government housing can be a substantial economic benefit.

Living on post can be extremely cost-effective because individuals living in government housing have no out-of-pocket expenses. They pay neither rent nor utilities. This is by far the most significant factor in giving service members the opportunity to earmark a generous portion of their monthly incomes for long-term investments.

BASIC ALLOWANCE FOR HOUSING (BAH)

Qualified military members who choose to reside off post receive a monthly housing allowance known as basic allowance for housing (BAH). The BAH is a monthly flat rate issued to qualified service members to be used for offpost housing. In general, the amount one receives for a BAH depends on location, rank, and number of dependents.

Recipients of the BAH who spend less on housing than the amount they receive do not have their allowance reduced.

Any remaining funds after all housing expenses are paid could potentially be invested.

In chapter 4, you'll read about Sergeant Major Austin: after a number of years of accumulating savings and a deployment during Desert Storm, he was able to pay cash to purchase his first home. This allowed him to direct his entitled BAH into his savings plan.

For further information regarding eligibility and the use of BAH, make an appointment at your unit's finance and housing departments.

HEALTH INSURANCE

A civilian retiring early will not qualify for government health care, such as Medicare. These civilians must then purchase health coverage with money taken from their retirement plans. This cost can be extremely high, depending on factors such as age and potential health problems they are experiencing. An individual retiring from the military has full medical coverage. This is not only a remarkable financial benefit, but it also gives service members valuable peace of mind.

THE MONTGOMERY GI BILL

On June 22, 1944, President Franklin Delano Roosevelt signed into law the Servicemen's Readjustment Act of 1944, commonly known as the GI Bill of Rights. It was revamped in 1984 by former Mississippi Congressman Gillespie V. "Sonny" Montgomery and has been known as the "Montgomery GI

Bill" ever since. This is possibly one of the most significant pieces of legislation pertaining to service members ever produced by the United States government.

The GI Bill is an education benefit earned through active duty, selected reserve, and National Guard service. The benefit is designed to help service members and eligible veterans cover the costs associated with getting an education or training. In 2008, due to the 9/11 events, the GI Bill was updated and enacted into law by Congress. For additional information, contact your unit's finance department.

PX/BX

Another military cost-saving advantage is shopping at the military exchange services, also known as the Post Exchange (PX) and Base Exchange (BX). The exchange can provide outstanding values that are only available to military personnel, saving their customers money. Savings on such items as groceries, electronics, and clothing can add up fast. Money saved can go directly into a retirement savings plan!

SHORT WORK COMMUTE (OR NONE AT ALL)

Living on base oftentimes allows military personnel to walk to work. Compare this to the average daily commute of most civilians. The amount you save in fuel costs could be directed into your investment plan. Some might think there is a negligible amount of money involved, but let's take a look.

A thirty-minute commute from the suburbs of a large city could easily be as far as twenty-five miles. If gasoline costs

$3.85 a gallon, a daily fifty-mile commute in a vehicle that gets twenty-five miles to the gallon will cost $100.00 or more each month. Comparatively, a service member who lives on base will pay next to nothing.

"I HAVE PLENTY OF TIME TO START SAVING— I'LL START SAVING LATER"

From a young person's perspective, this statement may appear to be a compelling argument. However, after investigating the arithmetic involved, it becomes apparent why exploiting the advantage of the time you have on your side early in your military career is a better option. But if you still think that you can make up for the time that is slipping away, please take a look at the following example, which illustrates the benefit of investing as much as you can—as early as you can.

Age of Investor	Years to Retiring at Age 65	APR	Initial Investment	Monthly Deposit	Amount of Savings
45	20	5%	$0.00	$450.00	$184,965.15
35	30	5%	$0.00	$450.00	$374,516.39
25	40	5%	$0.00	$450.00	$686,709.07
18	47	5%	$0.00	$450.00	$1,018,926.11

As you can see, time literally is money!

Chapter 3

Why Is Time So Important?

THE TIME VALUE OF MONEY AND THE POWER OF COMPOUNDING

Albert Einstein said that compound interest is one of the greatest mathematical concepts of our time. Compounding has also been called the eighth wonder of the world. Why? The power of compound interest can increase even a modest amount of money into a staggering sum that most people would find unbelievable.

The time value of money is the value of money figuring in a given amount of *interest* earned over a given amount of time. The time value of money is the central concept in finance theory. Lucky for you, by beginning your financial plan today, time is certainly on your side!

PUTTING YOUR MONEY TO WORK FOR YOU

As the saying goes, smart people put their money to work for them. How do they do it? It can be as simple as storing your money in a savings account. Deposits in a savings account earn interest. The more you save and the longer you save, the harder your money will work for you by earning interest. Let's take a look at a basic savings account.

For example, what if you placed a $1.00 bill into a box every day for forty years? By storing $365.00 per year for forty years, you will have accumulated $14,600.00.

But what would happen if you deposited that same single $1.00 bill in a savings account that earned 2% interest? Through the power of compounding, the same amount deposited would have earned an additional $7,433.07 for a grand total of $22,033.07. This is an elementary example of how the saying "putting your money to work for you" came about.

But before we continue, let's back up a moment and define some financial concepts that will explain how the concept of "putting your money to work for you" actually transpires.

WHAT IS PRINCIPAL?

By definition, the principal is the original amount of money you deposit into an interest-earning account.

WHAT IS INTEREST?

Interest is a fee paid to a depositor by a lending institution on borrowed capital. The concept is that the financial institution is "borrowing" money from you. The interest could be thought of as "rent" on the money you deposit in a bank or credit union. The amount of interest applied to the principal is referred to as the interest rate.

Two different types of interest can be offered by lending institutions: simple interest and compound interest. The differences between the two are explored in the next segment.

WHAT IS SIMPLE INTEREST?

With simple interest, the amount of the deposit does not change. The interest earned is paid directly to the depositor at the end of each determined interval of time. This interest is not added to the principal (the initial deposit). It is given to the depositor rather than placed into the account. If the owner of the savings account never added or withdrew funds after making the initial deposit, he or she would be paid the same amount of interest each interval.

AN EXAMPLE OF SIMPLE INTEREST OVER TEN YEARS

Let's say you deposit $1,000 in a savings account at a local credit union. The account earns 3% interest annually.

Years Passed	Account Balance	Percent Interest	Interest Earned
1	$1,000.00	3%	$30.00
2	$1,000.00	3%	$30.00
3	$1,000.00	3%	$30.00
4	$1,000.00	3%	$30.00
5	$1,000.00	3%	$30.00
6	$1,000.00	3%	$30.00
7	$1,000.00	3%	$30.00
8	$1,000.00	3%	$30.00
9	$1,000.00	3%	$30.00
10	$1,000.00	3%	$30.00
Total	**$1,000.00**		**$300.00**

At the end of each year, the $30 is paid to you, and you may reinvest it or choose not to.

WHAT IS COMPOUND INTEREST?

With compound interest, the interest that is earned over a set period of time, let's say a quarter of a year, is left in the account. This additional money will be included in future compounding along with the initial deposit. With compound interest, future interest is earned on the original principal *plus* the interest from the previous quarter.

In other words, compounding occurs when accumulated interest is declared to be part of the principal. In this way, the interest earned each quarter is figured on a larger amount of money than the quarter before. If you recall, earnings in a simple interest account are paid directly to the owner of the account, and not included in future compounding.

There are some determining factors that can affect the money earned. First of all, the amount you earn depends on the frequency with which interest is compounded. It may be compounded annually, quarterly, monthly, or daily. The amount of interest you are paid is also a determining factor, of course. In order to accurately define the amount to be paid under a legal contract, when you open an account your financial institution will clearly specify the interest rate and the frequency with which it is compounded.

AN EXAMPLE OF COMPOUND INTEREST OVER TEN YEARS

Again, we will say that you have deposited $1,000 in a local credit union at 3% interest.

Years Passed	Account Balance	Percent Interest	Interest Earned
1	$1,000.00	3%	$30.00
2	$1,030.00	3%	$30.09
3	$1,060.09	3%	$32.64
4	$1,092.73	3%	$32.79
5	$1,125.52	3%	$33.77
6	$1,159.29	3%	$34.78
7	$1,194.07	3%	$35.82
8	$1,229.89	3%	$36.90
9	$1,266.79	3%	$38.01
10	$1,304.80	3%	$39.15
Total	$1,343.95		$343.95

SIMPLE VS. COMPOUND INTEREST

Let's take one last look at simple and compound interest in these examples side by side.

Years Passed	Simple Interest: Interest Earned	Simple Interest: $ in Account	Compound Interest: Interest Earned	Compound Interest: $ in Account
1	$30.00	$1,000.00	$30.00	$1,030.00
2	$30.00	$1,000.00	$30.09	$1,060.09
3	$30.00	$1,000.00	$32.64	$1,092.73
4	$30.00	$1,000.00	$32.79	$1,125.52
5	$30.00	$1,000.00	$33.77	$1,159.29
6	$30.00	$1,000.00	$34.78	$1,194.07
7	$30.00	$1,000.00	$35.82	$1,229.89
8	$30.00	$1,000.00	$36.90	$1,266.79
9	$30.00	$1,000.00	$38.01	$1,304.80
10	$30.00	$1,000.00	$39.15	$1,343.95
Total:	**$300.00**	**$1,000.00**	**$343.95**	**$1,343.95**

When you compare the $300.00 earned with the simple interest account to the $343.95 in the compound interest account, you can see the additional $43.95 earned, and gain a visual perspective of the mathematics involved.

WHAT IS THE "RULE OF 72"?

The "Rule of 72" is a method for determining how fast money grows when earning a given interest rate. You simply divide 72 by your interest rate to find out how many years it will take for your money to double.

Let's use an 8% interest rate as an example: 72 ÷ 8 = 9 years.

So it will take nine years for your investment to double. This is merely an approximation, and it starts to break down at rates above 10%, but it will give you a general idea.

REEXAMINING THE TIME VALUE OF MONEY

When it comes to investing, time may be the most valuable element of your investment plan. You will soon realize how the mismanagement of time can have a devastating effect on your money.

The time value of money is based on the premise that an investor will most likely prefer to receive a fixed amount of money today rather than the same amount at some point in the future. The philosophy is that a dollar today is worth more than a dollar tomorrow; a dollar today can earn interest until the time you would have received the money in the future, which equals a larger sum. Therefore, common sense tells us that it is better to receive money sooner and invest in our future in order to take advantage of the accumulating interest.

For example, assuming a 3% interest rate, $100 that you invest today will be worth $103 in one year. But $100 that you receive today may be the equivalent of only $97 a year ago due to the interest opportunity you lost and inflation.

BIGGER NUMBERS

To see the tremendous impact of starting an early savings plan, let's look at the value of time from another perspective.

Consider a college graduate who, after paying off all outstanding student loans by the age of twenty-nine, manages to faithfully save $4,200.00 a year. If the college grad was fortunate enough to earn a 5.7% annual percentage rate (APR) until he or she chooses to retire at the age of sixty-five, it may be possible to accumulate $526,007.64.

On the other hand, with the ability to annually invest the same amount of $4,200.00 at the age of eighteen, an E1 private would amass $1,033,294.80 by the age of sixty-five. This is the dramatic effect of just a few extra years of compounded interest working for him or her.

This example is based on a 5.7% annual percentage rate of return. It is important to remember such a consistent return is by no means guaranteed. However, the example clarifies how saving as much as you can, as early as you can, will tremendously impact your ultimate goal.

Is it now apparent how a military recruit has a noticeable advantage of saving money during these early years? These are the same years that may unexpectedly slip past the average civilian. By creating a savings plan today and taking advantage of investing early, the additional time for interest to compound can clearly provide the service member a distinct advantage.

BOTTOM LINE WITH COMPOUND INTEREST

You now realize why it is so beneficial to start your investment plan as soon as you are able. The bottom line is: the younger the investor, the more distant retirement age is. The more distant retirement age is. the more advantageous compound interest is. That's it. Now when you hear your fellow service members say, "Oh, I'm young, I have plenty of time to worry about retirement," you can jump in there and educate them on their most valuable asset—time.

STILL NOT CONVINCED? LET'S LOOK AT ONE LAST SCENARIO.

In order for a forty-five-year-old chief executive officer of a Fortune 500 company to accrue $1,000,000.00 by age sixty-five, he would have to set aside $2,372.42 every single month, assuming a 6% APR.

How much would an eighteen-year-old private serving in the US military need to save to have roughly the same amount by age sixty-five? Only $350 a month, assuming a 6% APR!

Now is it becoming clear why saving and investing your hard-earned military pay as early as possible is such an advantage?

Chapter 4

Straight from the Top: A Firsthand Story with Financial Success

"My plan was simple, and I believe that is why it has been so successful for me."

Sergeant Major Austin
US Army (retired)

"Relax, as you were. Enjoy your breakfast," Sergeant Major Austin stated as he entered the crowded chow hall looking for a place to have a seat. The sleeves of his uniform were covered in dust, but his torso was clean where his body armor had spared him from the dirt and grime of the inner city of Baghdad. The skin around his eyes had distinct rings where his goggles had protected them from the filthy soot in the air. Holding his breakfast tray in one hand, he pulled out the empty chair directly across from Private Erickson and I with the other and sat down.

The sergeant major had joined our company on a mission the night before. Our unit had returned to the base, where we were quietly eating breakfast in the congested dining hall. Since our unit had arrived in Iraq only a few weeks prior, I decided to comment on our culinary options.

"Sergeant Major Austin, this chow is pretty good."

I was surprised by his response. "You know, back stateside, it is not uncommon for a fast-food lunch to be as high as seven or eight bucks. Over the past twenty-nine years, I have contributed nearly $90,000 toward my retirement plan just from eating at the chow hall or packing my own lunch."

"That's great, Sergeant Major," I said, without giving my response much thought. I continued munching on a piece of bacon.

"No, you don't get it, son," he said in the gruff, seasoned tone one acquires after decades as an enlistee. "Since this is my last deployment and I am about to retire, I am attempting to pass on this valuable information to as many fellow service members as I can. I'm sharing this with you not to boast about my own finances. I want to enlighten you with the tremendous financial advantage you have at your age. By investing your pay early and exploiting the amount of time you have on your side, your savings could potentially grow to a much greater amount than you may realize."

"Roger, Sergeant Major," I answered, wondering where this conversation was going. I lowered my bacon and paid more respect as he continued.

"Check this out," the sergeant major stated while leaning toward Private Erickson and me to ensure our attention. "A brand-new E-1 now earns well over $1,000 per month upon enlistment. After completing basic training, he or she already has $4,000 cash to salt away for his or her future. Some privates are only seventeen years old. Did you know that by the time that seventeen-year-old kid is fifty-eight, that same $4,000 could be worth over $40,000 if invested wisely? And that is without adding another penny."

"Wow, I had no idea," Private Erickson chimed in, looking bewildered. Ironically, Erickson used the exact same amount of money as a down payment on his brand-new SUV prior to our deployment.

The sergeant major continued, "I was the oldest of eight kids in our family. We grew up below the poverty level. Hungry and without a penny in my pocket, I proudly enlisted in the US Army as an infantryman when I was eighteen. Next year when I retire, I will have over half a million in cash, in addition to my military pension."

"Really? How is that possible, Sergeant Major?" I asked, thinking that many soldiers I knew were flat broke.

"I immediately formed a savings plan after my enlistment. My plan was simple, and I believe that is why it has been so successful for me. Beginning in 1976, I was able to save $200 per month. I was young, unfamiliar with personal finance, and unable to take the time to explore investment options. So, I simply placed the money into a mutual fund recommended by a captain at my unit's financial office. I have used this very same mutual fund throughout my entire military career because of its conservative risk and consistent earning potential. As the years passed, I gradually increased my monthly savings. Currently, I deposit about $1,600 per month."

"It must have been hard not spending that money, Sergeant Major," Private Erickson said.

"Yes, I made some sacrifices along the way. But whatever it was that I managed to get by without, certainly will make my life more enjoyable next year when I retire. Hell, I'll only be fifty years old. Based on today's pay scale, the combat pay you guys receive during this deployment, and generous reenlistment bonuses, you could achieve the same goal in considerably less time. If you two grunts have any sense, you will take this information to heart and begin your own financial plans today."

SERGEANT MAJOR AUSTIN'S PLAN, BASED ON THE 2008 MILITARY PAY SCALE

I researched military pay scales dating back to 1976 to determine how the sergeant major was able to accumulate $500,000 during his thirty-three-year career. I then compared the pay scales from thirty-three years ago to the 2008 pay scale, using the same savings percentage as the sergeant major. Let's see how the numbers compare.

The sergeant major initiated his investment plan with $1,000 he earned while completing basic training in 1976. After this, he was able to save $200 per month. This equates to 53% of his monthly pay. (In our example, we will use 50%.) He increased the dollar amount of savings every three years, based on promotions, pay raises, etc.

He advised us that he had placed the funds into a conservative-risk mutual fund that earned an average of 4% interest over the next thirty-three years. Although financial advisors certainly recommend more than a single investment tool to diversify risk, for the sergeant major it proved to be a relatively safe investment and, fortunately, provided a steady return for him.

Since this is an approximation, our example will increase the monthly savings every three years based on the pay scale for the year specified. We'll use 4% interest throughout the example.

Year	Rank	Monthly Pay	Monthly Savings	Accumulated Funds
1975	-	$0.00	$0.00	$1000 basic training pay
1976-78	E1	$374.40	$200.00	$8,763.58
1979-81	E3	$475.50	$300.00	$21,333.41
1982-84	E4	$888.60	$400.00	$39,321.18
1985-87	E5	$1,086.30	$500.00	$63,416.44
1988-90	E6	$1,464.60	$700.00	$98,214.66
1991-93	E7	$1,820.40	$900.00	$145,078.03
1994-96	E7	$2,124.60	$1,000.00	$201,723.95
1997-99	E8	$2,639.70	$1,200.00	$273,215.61
2000-02	E8	$3,295.50	$1,500.00	$365,260.62
2003-05	E9	$4,757.40	$2,000.00	$488,111.15
2006-09	E9	$5,394.00	$2,500.00	$645,687.88

Now here is the really good news: when we base Sergeant Major Austin's 50% savings plan on the 2007 military pay scale, accumulating $500,000.00 is substantially more feasible. Since we are unable to predict what the military pay scale will be in the future, we will simply use the lowest pay issued on the 2007 pay scale throughout our entire thirty-three-year example. In 2007, an E-1 earned a monthly income of $1,178.10. Again, for the purposes of this example, we'll use the conservative annual percentage rate of 4%.

Years of Career	Initial Savings	Annual Percentage Return	Monthly Savings	Potential Investment Growth
2007-2040	$4000.00 basic training pay	4%	$600.00	$507,279.21

Keep in mind that both of these savings plans only consider deposits from the income of a service member's basic monthly pay. They do not include money received from reenlistment bonuses, combat pay, overseas pay, Basic Allowance for Housing (BAH), etc., all of which the sergeant major advised that he had salted away in addition to his monthly savings. The addition of funds such as these would increase the calculations, making the results much greater.

Chapter 5

Why Are Financial Investments So Mysterious?

WHERE DO I BEGIN?

Just by reading the few preceding chapters, you may realize why it is beneficial for you to start a savings plan today. The next step is the creation of your own financial plan. But where do you begin? Creating your plan may seem intimidating, overwhelming, and even somewhat of a mystery. On the contrary, preparing a plan to secure your finances is not a mystery at all. In fact, it is a matter of organization, dedication, and simple arithmetic. After learning some additional concepts in the upcoming chapters, you will realize that accumulating a substantial nest egg for retirement is basically a combination of:

- Organizing your resources and establishing a budget
- Education regarding different investment tools
- Self-discipline to dedicate a portion of your income to your savings plan
- Time for your financial portfolio to grow

A CONSERVATIVE INVESTMENT STRATEGY VS. PRIVATE ERICKSON'S NEW CAR PURCHASE

From an investor's point of view, purchasing a new car is a terrible investment, but what's worse is purchasing a new car using credit. Let's take a look at what Private Erickson could have done with the money he used to purchase his new SUV. In the following examples, we'll assume that a $10,000 initial investment is feasible, because that is the amount Erickson used as a down payment. Also, we'll use a conservative 4% annual percentage rate.

Months of Accumulation	APR	Initial Investment	Monthly Deposit	Account Balance
72	4%	$10,000.00	$0.00	$12,707.42

In the above example, we see that if Private Erickson had chosen to invest his $10,000.00 deposit for the same seventy-two months during which he was obligated to repay the lending institution, he would have seen his account grow to $12,707.42. That is an additional $2,707.42 that he didn't have before. Not too bad.

Years of Accumulation	APR	Initial Investment	Monthly Deposit	Account Balance
46	4%	$10,000.00	$0.00	$62,773.01

By the retirement age of sixty five, the same $10,000.00 had the potential to accumulate to $60,000.00 with a 4% annual percentage rate. That's $50,000.00 that he did not have before. Even better.

Months of Accumulation	APR	Initial Investment	Monthly Deposit	Account Balance
72	4%	$10,000.00	$700.00	$69,56.21

If Private Erickson had invested the seventy-two payments of $700 per month in addition to the initial $10,000, his balance had the potential to grow to nearly $70,000. Think about that for a moment. In six years the new vehicle's value will diminish to a fraction of its initial cost. On the other hand, if Private Erickson had chosen the investment plan, he would have had the confidence that he was well on his way to a much-deserved early retirement.

Years of Accumulation	APR	Initial Investment	Monthly Deposit	Account Balance
46	4%	$10,000.00	$700.00	$1,171,006.25

The results would have been even more impressive if Erickson had invested the monthly payment of $700 per month in addition to the initial $10,000 until the age of sixty-five. Yes, you're reading that correctly.

At 4% interest his investment portfolio had the potential to grow to $1,171,006.25—over $1 million! What a difference investing early can make!

When purchasing a new vehicle, many times the salesperson will only focus on the amount of the monthly payment "you can afford." The salesperson may not mention that an automobile is a depreciating asset. As it ages, it loses value rapidly and drastically. To complete the sale, explanations of the costly expenses to operate the vehicle are overlooked. High-interest loans, processing fees, and taxes are sometimes not clearly explained until the salesperson is asking you to sign the paperwork. After the sale is complete, the new owner has to be able to insure, repair, maintain, and register the vehicle with the state, further driving the cost of your new investment higher. To avoid these costly oversights, strongly consider purchasing an automobile only when you can pay cash for it.

TEMPTATION

Unfortunately Private Erickson and so many others like him learn the pitfalls of personal finance the hard way. Purchases that seem like an excellent idea at the time may not always be in our best interest for the long term. The ability to overcome the temptation to purchase lavish and unnecessary material items can be an invaluable trait. If you are able to do so, the odds of your financial success will increase immensely. Living a comfortable lifestyle during your retirement is nothing more than a dream if you do not have the ability to accrue savings and build your investment portfolio. It will be necessary to learn to recognize and steer clear of excessive purchases.

Avoiding tempting purchases may seem overwhelming at first. Forgoing temptations, both large and small, requires tremendous willpower. Let's face it: now, more than ever, there are material items available to us that seem almost necessary. Many individuals find avoiding such purchases the most difficult part of building a secure financial future. With liberal lines of credit available, even the lack of cash is not a barrier anymore.

In addition to vehicles, items such as boats, ATVs, computers, snow mobiles, electronics, even exercise equipment can be purchased on credit. I recently saw a television commercial for a rotisserie oven that could be purchased for "three easy installments of $29.95." Think about how ridiculous that is. If it is necessary for you to have a payment plan for a kitchen appliance, that may be an indication that you cannot afford it.

The point is that a purchase on credit is not free money. On the contrary, an item purchased on credit comes at an even greater price. Unfortunately the price is often in the form of outrageous interest rates, penalties, late fees, and ultimately damage to your credit score.

PENNIES ADD UP TO DOLLARS

When it comes to saving money, those pennies can add up fast. If you think the difference between making your own sandwich from items you purchased at the grocery store and eating lunch at a trendy sandwich restaurant is only a few dollars, try looking at it from an annual perspective. By looking at the bigger picture, you can clearly see why those dollars add up.

For example, if you are able to save $4 every day by making your own sandwich, multiply that amount by 365 and see how much you can save in a year. You no longer saved just $4; now you can see that in one year you saved $1,400—quite a chunk!

A financial calculator enables you to predict with a fair amount of accuracy that if you save this amount annually for twenty years at a 6% annual percentage rate, you have the potential of accumulating over $50,000.

Chapter 6

Continue to Educate Yourself

"Learn the basics first, and you'll accomplish any financial goals you set for yourself."

Captain Grant
US Coast Guard

My name is Samuel Grant and I've served in the US Coast Guard for thirteen years. Prior to my initial enlistment, I graduated with a bachelor's degree in engineering. Currently, I perform a relatively high-tech job as a captain piloting an HH-60J Jayhawk. Can you imagine performing this job but somehow not having the ability to balance a checkbook? Well, it's true.

I had taken one accounting course for my engineering degree, but none of that information covered the basics, like establishing a budget. My wife and I actually met with the branch manager of our bank and asked her to teach us how to read our monthly bank statement.

Now we realize that one of our biggest obstacles was our lack of understanding about the basic concepts of investing money and the tools used to do so. So we decided to do something about it. We checked out numerous personal finance books at the library.

Then, we made an appointment with a reputable, professional financial advisor. The advisor answered our questions thoroughly. He explained that the majority of his clients were novices, just like my wife and I. He described how many of his clients had avoided investing altogether because they did not understand the elementary ideas of investing. "To continuously make money," he explained, "you must be financially literate." After my wife and I met with our advisor several more times, we started applying the information to our lifestyle. We were now living well below our combined income. We saved a great deal of money with our frugal lifestyle, and placed 20% of our annual salaries into our diversified investments.

With a little luck, we plan to retire in our midfifties, at which time we'll have accumulated more money in our accounts than we ever thought was possible.

Our strategy was simple. When my wife and I did not know how to invest our savings, we found someone we could trust to show us how. Investing and personal finance can be intimidating. But truthfully, all it takes to succeed is a little self-education. Learn the basics first, and you'll accomplish any financial goals you set for yourself.

Chapter 7

Basic Training: Necessary for Military Success *and* Organizing Financial Documentation

This chapter, like the basic training you received when you entered the military, will cover the basics of organizing your financial documentation. Becoming organized will ensure the success of your financial plan.

As you organize your finances, you will gain confidence with the security that doing so brings. You work hard for your military pay. Enjoy knowing that you're making the most of it!

Organizing your personal finances will:

- Ensure that your bills are paid on time
- Help you avoid late fees
- Help you avoid debt
- Instill confidence knowing you're in control
- Equip you to thoroughly prepare tax statements
- Help you attain financial goals
- Promote confidence

Disorganized handling of your finances can lead to:

- Loss of receipts
- Late bill payment—or failure to pay bills at all
- Loss of assets—including cash
- Borrowing funds to meet obligations
- Endless searches for lost tax documentation
- Damaged credit rating
- Unnecessary frustration

RECORD KEEPING: WHERE DO I BEGIN?

It is a fact that creating a filing system that works for you will prevent you from wasting valuable time and money. You'll begin by identifying any problems you recognize in your current system. Then you will implement strategies to help you overcome your concerns. In addition, you'll find new techniques to further streamline your record-keeping system. The system you use will likely evolve over time through trial and error.

Structuring your personal finances will allow you to track your spending, organize your tax return information ahead of time, and effectively store documentation for the appropriate period of time.

KEEP IT SIMPLE

If you are just starting out, try not to make your system too elaborate. To begin, a basic routine is what you are attempting to accomplish. If your methods become too complex, it will be hard for you to maintain them. The following will help you develop a system similar to the one I have found to work best for me.

WHAT YOU'LL NEED TO START:

- Two large plastic file boxes
- Twelve to twenty-four hanging file folders

In the first file box, you can store your tax documentation. You will keep all of your other financial documentation in the second. I use inexpensive plastic file boxes because they are easily portable and have more than enough room inside. You can find them at any office supply store or large all-purpose store. Hanging file folders are sold anywhere you can find file boxes. Be sure to purchase hanging folders that include labels.

Basic Training 39

DOCUMENTATION TO CONSIDER STORING:

- Insurance policies
- Investment paperwork
- Banking documentation
- Credit statements
- Bill stubs
- Paycheck stubs
- Receipts for large or expensive items
- Mortgage papers
- Passports
- Car titles
- Stock certificates
- Annual IRA (individual retirement account) information
- Pension statements

STEPS TO ORGANIZING YOUR DOCUMENTATION:

1. Begin by sorting all the financial papers you believe to be relevant at this point. If you are unsure whether you should save something, it is best to save it just in case.
2. Separate your documents into piles according to their purpose. Organize them chronologically.
3. Label the file folders and place them in your file boxes.
4. Place each pile in the appropriate file folder.

This system may seem ridiculously simple—because it is. At this point, you are just starting out, and keeping it simple will eliminate frustration and ensure your success.

HOW LONG SHOULD I STORE MY DOCUMENTATION?

Part of organizing your records is determining:

- Which documents need to be kept
- How long you should keep the documents
- What can be thrown away

Different people have different opinions on this subject. When you begin the process, you may find the following guidelines helpful. They have worked well for me.

Document	How Long to Keep It
Tax returns and other tax forms	I keep mine indefinitely. Others keep them for seven years because this is how long the IRS has to perform an audit. Keep a separate file for each year.
Property records	Keep property records as long as you own the property they pertain to.
Receipts/warranties	This depends on the items purchased. Use your own judgment.
401(k) and IRA statements	I keep my quarterly statements until I receive my annual statement, and then shred them. I keep my annual statements indefinitely.
Brokerage statements	I keep these indefinitely for tax purposes.

Mutual fund statements	I keep these indefinitely for tax purposes.
Credit card statements	Keep them for each annual tax file.
Pay stubs	I suggest keeping pay stubs until you receive your W-2 and then shredding them.
Retirement/savings plan statements	I keep the quarterly statements until I receive the annual statement. I then shred the quarterlies and keep the annual statements indefinitely.
Bank records	Keep them in your annual tax files.
Bills	I shred bills after I have checked the canceled check online. You may consider keeping bills for insured items such as jewelry, appliances, electronics, and collectibles in case you need to file an insurance claim.

Again, the preceding is an example of what I have practiced for years. This system has worked well for me. If you choose, you can simply use this information as a guide to design your own record-keeping system. The main idea is to find a system that works well for you.

WHY SHOULD I STORE MY TAX RECORDS IN SEPARATE BOXES?

This may not be necessary for you now, especially if you are just beginning to save your records. I started out including my tax documentation in the same box as all my other records and eventually created a separate file system because of the convenience it provided.

My tax box now contains information from every year for the past twenty years. The files are separated by year and include W-2s, 1099s, receipts, tax returns, and any other tax information that pertains to a particular year.

BE PATIENT

Remember, there is no single right or wrong way to organize your financial information. Doing so will require patience until you find a system that works for you. The organization and development of your record-keeping system will take some time and dedication, but the peace of mind you will have afterward will make it well worth your effort.

Chapter 8

Self-Made Millionaire

"In my opinion, I have the income equivalent of a millionaire."

Colonel Walsh
US Marine Corps (retired)

As individuals, we all envision our retirements differently. I found the vision of retiring Marine Corps Regiment Commander Colonel Walsh, particularly interesting. With a long-term outlook, his philosophy was that just a fraction of a service member's paycheck can snowball into a substantial amount if handled properly.

Colonel Walsh planned to retire two years after his final deployment to Afghanistan in 2007. Although he did not have a million dollars in cash in the bank, it was his opinion that he would have the income equivalency of a millionaire.

He explained that his savings consisted of nearly $300,000; from a portion of that, he would earn approximately 2.25% in low-risk money-market funds and approximately 1.75% in CDs that were insured by the Federal Deposit Insurance Corporation (FDIC). In addition, he would begin to receive his annual pension of over $40,000 after retirement.

Colonel Walsh's philosophy was that the interest from his low-risk investments, in addition to his annual pension, equated to the amount of interest he would have gained from having a million dollars cash in the bank. The icing on his cake was that he had saved an additional $200,000 over his thirty-year career in the military to pay cash for the construction of a new home after his retirement.

Colonel Walsh made it clear he was not claiming to be a financial expert. His outlook was based on an informal opinion regarding his own net worth. But, now that Colonel Walsh is settled into his new home on his horse farm in Kentucky, I am sure he is quite pleased with the foresight he used in accomplishing his goals.

FORESIGHT

"Foresight" is defined as perception of the significance and nature of events before they have occurred; care in providing for the future; and the act of looking forward. Military personnel like Marine Corps Colonel Walsh who have the ability to envision their livelihood in the future are likely to achieve financial success. Foresight can assist investors in achieving both short- and long-term goals and motivate them while they are doing so.

In other words, individuals who have the ability to envision where they will be in five, ten, thirty, or even sixty years find it much easier to adjust their current lifestyles and reach their goals.

CHAPTER 9

HOW DO YOU ENVISION YOUR LIFESTYLE DURING RETIREMENT?

The first step in figuring out how much money you will need during retirement is to think about what you will be doing at that time of your life. For some people, retirement is a time to do all the things they were unable to do while working. For others, it is a time for leisure and rest. For most, it is somewhere in between.

To begin, ask yourself this simple question: "What type of lifestyle do I want to have when I stop working?" Every service member's answer will be different. Your unique answer will determine the amount of money you will need.

Maybe you have a list of things you have always wanted to do, but you've been too busy working—things like traveling or pursuing hobbies.

Will your retirement lifestyle increase the amount you spend? To support these costs, will it be necessary to have an income greater than your monthly paycheck? Perhaps you picture yourself enjoying your free time leisurely reading books and engaging in less-extravagant recreational activities near your hometown. By doing so, you may actually spend less money than you do now.

The key is preparing a financial plan today that will support the lifestyle you anticipate in your future. If your savings plan today will not support your retirement, you may need to significantly alter your current lifestyle. If your current plan supports your future endeavors, saving money for retirement should be relatively easy for you.

HOW DO I MAKE SURE I CAN AFFORD TO HAVE THE LIFESTYLE I WANT?

That is a good question. And fortunately, the answer is simple. Your current financial plan should balance your income and your lifestyle. That's it.

For example, early in your working career, if you choose to use a large portion of your monthly income to mortgage a luxury car, much less of your money will be available for savings. The result could be a longer career than you'd like or less money when you retire—or both. Defining and maintaining your balance is the key to reaching the goals you envision.

Determining a financial plan that works best for you is based upon knowing where your future is headed. So, whether retirement is forty years away or forty weeks, start by mapping out some of your broader retirement goals.

To do so, the following are some thoughts to consider:

- At what age do you plan to retire?
- How much time do you have until you reach that age?
- Are you planning to retire completely or continue working part time?
- Will your projected savings meet your needs?

After you have determined the answers to these questions, you can begin to fine-tune your plan for attaining them.

A MILLION DOLLARS SHOULD BE ENOUGH—RIGHT?

Professional advisors estimate that the average retired person requires 60% to 80% of his or her last year's working income to maintain an equivalent lifestyle after retirement. Calculating the amount of income you believe will be necessary to support your retirement lifestyle allows you to structure your current savings plan. Figuring this out today will give you a rough estimate of how much money you really need for tomorrow.

The fact is, if you are frugal enough to live on the interest alone from $1 million, you could anticipate an income between $20,000 and $40,000 annually. Although this is a respectable amount, it only goes as far as inflation, your lifestyle, and your health will allow it to go. Without any debt, this conservative amount may or may not provide a comfortable lifestyle. For others who envision a life of luxury, this amount will likely not be enough.

Take a look at your current expenses. If you think these will be the same once you retire, it's easy to figure out what income you will need to have later. And if you suspect that you will be spending more, or less, after retirement, you can plan accordingly.

DEVELOPING YOUR OWN FORESIGHT

Take a moment to think of the purchases you have made over the past few years, both large and small. Then consider whether they were worth the money you spent on them.

Be honest with yourself when asking the following questions:

- Could I have gotten by just as well with purchasing a used version or perhaps a less luxurious one?
- Could I have bought a smaller amount of something rather than the supersize?
- Could I have avoided the more expensive name brand and purchased the generic version?

Taking some time to reflect on how you could have handled your money differently is a healthy thing to do. Learning from past experiences can certainly benefit your future.

Imagine if the cash from excessive spending in the past were in your bank account today accumulating interest—what a feeling that would be!

Now, imagine yourself five years in the future. Based on your current spending habits, can you picture your financial situation at that point? This is a simple but effective approach to predicting similar feelings after making future purchases.

Learn from your past, but don't dwell on it. Evaluate your past spending habits and recognize what you could have done differently. Then keep moving forward. That's what having superior foresight is all about.

DETERMINING YOUR GOALS

In chapter 14, you'll read about distinguishing the things you need in life from the things you want. Now, you will learn to define your goals. Establishing goals and preparing a plan to meet them will ensure that you can build a financially sound future.

Take a moment to envision the specifics of your future. In Colonel Walsh's case, he envisioned himself living on a horse farm in Kentucky, with plenty of money in his savings account to support his military pension—a specific goal. A specific goal will give you a focal point. A distinct goal can also give you something to look forward to. In a sense, the goal could be seen as a reward for handling your finances responsibly. And once you have a specific goal in mind, you'll know exactly what you need, and you can develop a financial plan aimed specifically at achieving that goal. The best way to do so is to look at your goal and come up with short-term, medium-term, and long-term goals that will help you get there.

Short-term goals:

These are things you can start doing now that are attainable within one year, such as:

- Creating a $1,000 emergency fund
- Paying off, or at least beginning to pay off, all credit card debt
- Reducing spending by $150 a month

Medium-term goals:

These take a little longer, but they are goals that you can reasonably meet within the next five years, such as:

- Funding a six-month emergency fund
- Making a down payment on a home
- Paying cash for a quality preowned vehicle

Long-term goals:

These get you where you want to be in your retirement, such as:

- Owning your home, debt free
- Building a retirement account large enough that the interest will support you
- Having cash to pay for your children's education

All of these are examples of financial goals that you *can* attain, but they won't happen on their own. Each one requires extensive planning, conservative living, and follow-through. The good news is that with a good strategy in place and the discipline to avoid costly temptations, you can attain them easily and with little stress.

Once you've decided what your goals are, it's time to map out the route that's going to get you to them.

CHARTS: VALUABLE TOOLS IN OUTLINING YOUR GOALS

The following chart is an example that provides a visual perspective in addition to giving you a more understandable way to set your goals. In this way, you can see them all together, on paper. You will quickly be able to see what is feasible and what will not work within the constraints of your monthly budget. The chart will allow you to routinely adjust the numbers to reflect your current situation, particularly if you create it in a spreadsheet.

By routinely monitoring your progress, you may find that your long-term goals are negatively affecting the attainability of your short-term goals, or vice versa. You might find, however, that you are living well within your means and can set even loftier short- or long-term goals. With this information, you can readjust your funds to work to your advantage.

How Do You Envision Your Lifestyle During Retirement?

Let's take a look at an example:

Financial Goal	Time Required to Reach Goal	Goal Amount	Interest Paid or Earned	Necessary Monthly Budgeted Amount
Pay off credit card balance	12 months	$2,600.00	-13%	$233.00
Pay off vehicle loan	36 months	$8,000.00	-8%	$251.00
Down payment for first home	5 years	$20,000.00	+2%	$320.00
Children's college fund	18 years	$50,000.00	+3%	$180.00
Retirement savings	30 years	$500,000.00	+4.6%	$650.00
Total Monthly Savings				$1,524.00

SETTING YOUR GOALS

"I want to have a lot of money when I retire" is an excellent idea. However, it is completely ineffective as a goal. It isn't specific. An example of a clearly stated goal is: I would like to accumulate $250,000 in the next twenty-five years, by the time I retire from the military at age forty-five.

It is much easier to devise a plan using your current and projected income if you state a specific, clear goal. If you establish your goals firmly before you create a specific plan for achieving them, you may find out early on that certain goals are not feasible, or discover that you can set even higher goals than you anticipated.

DON'T GET DISCOURAGED

As you run your own numbers for a specific goal, it may become apparent that your vision of the future has a distinct possibility of becoming reality. On the other hand, you may see that you need to reconsider expectations that are too lofty and set your sights on more a realistic objective. If the latter is the case, don't get discouraged. You are very fortunate to have found out early enough in your life that you can still make adjustments and find a way to accomplish your ambitions. Either way, you will soon discover that if you save as much as possible, as early as possible, you will be off to an excellent start.

Chapter 10

Off to a Great Start

"My money is doing exactly what it should be doing—working for me."

Private First Class Kennedy
US Army Infantryman

Private First Class Kennedy had recently completed basic training and volunteered to be sent directly to our unit in Iraq. His decision to do so said a great deal about his character. He was assigned to our squad during the final few months of our deployment.

During downtime, one of Private First Class Kennedy's favorite topics was how he had begun to invest his money before he deployed. He had always intended to make the military his career and anticipated his military pension upon retirement. However, in addition to the valuable pension, he recognized the benefit of investing early as a significant supplement.

To begin his education, he had checked out numerous books from the on-post library regarding personal finance. Next, he contacted an investment company that specialized in working with members of the military and their families.

Private First Class Kennedy's investment plan was simple; far from complex. He prioritized the establishment of an emergency fund while simultaneously eliminating his credit card debt. Afterwards, he began to divert a portion of his monthly income into the Military Thrift Savings Life Cycle Plan, a Roth IRA, and a mutual stock fund (defined in upcoming chapters). While deployed, he took advantage of the Military Savings Deposit Program.

PRIVATE FIRST CLASS KENNEDY'S PLAN INCLUDED THE FOLLOWING ELEMENTS:

- A checking account
- A savings account for general funds
- A savings account for emergencies
- Three or four $1,000 CDs
- Use of the military's Savings Deposit Program while on deployment
- Use of the Military Thrift Savings Life Cycle Plan
- A Roth IRA
- A Mutual Stock Index Fund

Private First Class Kennedy considers his financial plan a complete success and is excited about how well his money is working for him. His money is doing exactly what he wants it to. Since he is working with an investment company instead of researching companies on his own, he feels as though his plan is on autopilot, leaving him with little to worry about.

Private First Class Kennedy attributes his success to the simplicity of his plan. There is no doubt that his patience, foresight, and determination will pay off for him for the rest of his life.

If you share Private First Class Kennedy's interest in investments and you want more information on military investment plans, visit the staff at your unit's finance department. You'll likely find they are more than willing to help you—and the information is free!

CHAPTER 11

MAKING A TENTATIVE PLAN

WHAT IS A BUDGET?

To effectively become financially successful, it will be necessary to develop a personal budget. A personal budget is an estimation of your income and expenses over a specified period of time. It can be viewed as an individual financial plan that distributes future income toward expenses, debt, savings, and investments.

The information you need to make a budget includes past spending in addition to known future income and expense obligations. A well-planned budget will provide the framework for living within your means and will also tell you how much you can designate for savings each month. Your financial success will greatly increase after establishing a budget.

Plan on establishing your budget based upon your pay periods. Typically, service members are paid bimonthly. Most often, your bills will be due at different times of the month. Begin by writing down each of your monthly bills to eliminate any surprises.

As time goes by, you can fine-tune your budget. For example, your utility bills may increase when you purchase a home. You can simply increase the amount budgeted for this monthly expense.

On the other hand, your income will fluctuate when you are promoted to a higher rank, receive a reenlistment bonus, or eliminate the debt that has been dragging you down. These surplus funds could be added to your emergency fund, or perhaps to your long-term investment portfolio.

While starting out, remember that handling your finances appropriately is part of a long-term lifestyle you want to live, and your initial attempt to budget your money does not have to be perfect. Your goal should be to establish the simplest budget to assure yourself that you are living within your means and not acquiring additional debt.

CREATING YOUR OWN BUDGET

Budgets oftentimes are too complex or time consuming to create and maintain. A software program can be a good way to get organized. However, specialty budget software can also be extremely detailed and tedious because of the extensive categorization it provides. If this occurs, the creator may become discouraged and give up entirely or, even worse, cause the individual to fall further backward in debt.

To avoid this, simplify your plan. With time, you'll discover that a simple budget can reduce stress and eliminate the need for complicated tracking schemes. An efficient budget may require about fifteen to twenty minutes per week.

ESTABLISHING YOUR OWN BUDGET STEP BY STEP

Step 1: Determine your income.

First, you need to confirm exactly how much income you receive each month. This includes your monthly salary, of course, as well as any additional supplemental income you may receive from a second job, investments, combat pay, housing allowance, enlistment bonuses, etc.

Step 2: Determine your expenses.

This task may prove to be more difficult. It is necessary to determine exactly how much you spend each month. Larger, fixed expenses, such as mortgages, vehicle payments, insurance, and utilities, are simple to track. Smaller, nonfixed expenses, such as gas, eating in restaurants, and entertainment, are a little more challenging. Track them for a few months and use the average to determine your expenses.

Step 3: Calculate your surplus cash.

In this step, you'll determine how much you'll be able to earmark for savings each month. Simply subtract your monthly expenses, determined in step two, from your monthly income, determined in step one. The remaining amount is the amount you can save. An ideal target for savings would be 40% of your overall income.

Remember, saving money is not an exact science, and you can increase or decrease the amount you save as your life circumstances change. The most important part is to begin saving now, no matter how much or how little you can afford to save.

Step 4: Prioritize the establishment of an emergency fund.

An emergency fund is intended to absorb large, unanticipated expenses that come up from time to time. Examples could include:

- Automobile collision
- Home fire
- Accidents
- Flood
- Unforeseen medical expenses
- Death in the family

Having such a fund will prevent you from going into debt should something of this nature occur in your life. Later in the book, we'll discuss in greater detail how to establish your emergency fund.

Step 5: Pay cash.

Becoming a cash-only person can bring a feeling of empowerment. Every pay period (bimonthly), I make a withdrawal from an ATM for enough cash to last me the next two weeks. Why? The reason is simple: with cash, I don't need to worry about overspending or tracking how much is left in that category. I use the cash to pay for gas, groceries, and entertainment. Entertainment can be anything, such as books, movies, fishing tackle, etc. By withdrawing these cash allotments twice a month, I know at a glance how much I have left until payday. This system virtually eliminates the use of a debit or credit card. Also, any cash left over from one pay period can be rolled over to the next. By doing so, it may not be necessary to withdraw the full amount allotted from the ATM. This system can become extremely gratifying—give it a try!

Step 6: Pay off and cut up your credit cards.
Credit cards typically charge high interest and can possibly promote overspending. Unless you were in a dire emergency, why would you use a credit card anyway? Purchases on credit cards are usually used for smaller items. If you can't pay cash for the smaller item, why would you use a credit card to buy it? You obviously cannot afford the item!

If you must have a credit card, simplify by having just one. Leave the card at home in a safe location and bring it with you only when you absolutely need it—while traveling, for example.

WHEN FIRST DESIGNING YOUR BUDGET, USE AS FEW BUDGET CATEGORIES AS POSSIBLE.

Some folks may disagree and recommend complicated systems with lots of different categories. However, when you are just beginning to get organized, I suggest trying to keep your method as simple as possible. This way, you won't waste your time juggling money in several categories.

USE A BASIC ELECTRONIC SPREADSHEET.

For many, the easiest way to establish a budget is through the use of an electronic worksheet. My basic electronic spreadsheet contains columns for income and expenses. I've created a simple formula that adds up the totals of each column of numbers. I start by listing my income and my monthly expense obligations. After considering my larger monthly expenses, I try to include just the basics, such as food, gas, and general entertainment. This technique keeps me organized and takes no time at all to adjust as income changes and expenses occur.

Let's take a look at a relatively simple example on the following page.

Income	Proposed	Actual	% of income
Military pay	$1,000.00	$1,081.32	
Other income	$0.00	$0.00	
Total Income	**$1,000.00**	**$1,081.32**	
Fixed Expenses			
Cell phone	$50.00	$48.92	5%
Credit card	$60.00	$58.50	6%
Auto insurance	$90.00	$89.66	9%
Internet	$60.00	$59.99	6%
Total Fixed Expenses	**$260.00**	**$257.07**	**26%**
Variable Expenses			
Food/personal	$150.00	$149.45	15%
Gas	$50.00	$48.41	5%

Entertainment	$65.00	$64.67	7%
Utilities	$75.00	$73.18	7%
Total Variable Expenses	$340.00	$335.71	34%
Total Expenses	$600.00	$592.78	60%
Remaining in Budget	$400.00	$408.76	40%

USING AUTOMATIC BILL PAY

When establishing my own budget, I set up electronic automatic withdrawals to pay bills from my checking account whenever possible.

Examples of bills that can be paid automatically each month include:

- Utilities
- Rent
- Mortgage
- Cell phone
- Internet
- Auto loan

After setting up the automatic payments online, the bills are routinely paid with virtually no effort. I have the peace of mind that the bills will be paid on time and save myself the expense and effort of writing and mailing checks to numerous obligations each month.

Chapter 12

Budget Examples

There are many strategies, systems, and techniques you can use to structure your budget. The following examples are a few of my favorites. These examples are time proven, simple to use, and can be powerful tools when applied. Let's look at the different examples and try to determine if any would work for you.

THE ENVELOPE SYSTEM

This is a budgeting system that has been around for a long time. The technique may even have been used by your grandparents, since it is based on using cash to pay for the majority of goods and services, rather than a debit or credit card. Although this is an old-fashioned system, it can be extremely effective because it is simple and it works. It also works well for those who have the tendency to use a credit card for impulsive purchases without giving the cost of the item a second thought.

Let's take a look at the steps you need to take for an effective envelope system:

1. Determine the amount of money required to pay your monthly bills.
2. Decide how much money from each paycheck you will deposit into savings.
3. Decide how much you can allow for each of your other predetermined categories.

    For example, I use four envelopes for:
    - Groceries
    - Clothing
    - Gas
    - Entertainment

4. Determine the spending cash allotted for each category.

    For example:
    - $200 groceries
    - $100 clothing
    - $75 gas
    - $50 entertainment

5. Then simply place in each envelope the predetermined amount of cash you intend to spend, and use it for the designated expense.

When you have spent the cash from any given envelope, there is no more available for that pay period, thus eliminating the possibility of overspending. If you have extra money in any of the envelopes at the end of the month, you can save it to increase the amount you get to spend the following month.

Or you can remove it from the envelope and put it in savings. That's it. Simple and effective. Right?

As an example, let's take a look at a trip to the supermarket. Before I leave, I'll count the available funds in my groceries envelope. By doing so, I'll know ahead of time how much budgeted money is available when I shop. When I'm ready to check out, I use the cash from the designated envelope to pay the cashier. Afterward, with a quick glance I can easily see how much money is available for the remaining time period. If there is no money remaining, I have the option to transfer cash from one envelope to another. This would eliminate the need to adjust my overall budget. How simple is that?

A SUMMARY OF THE ENVELOPE SYSTEM:

1. **Budget each paycheck.**

   A tight budget is a must if you're going to successfully implement the envelope system.

2. **Work out your budget on a spreadsheet.**

   You may have already completed this step based on the previous information in this chapter. With the envelope system, you'll find that the more accurate your budget is on your spreadsheet, the more effective your envelope system will be.

3. **Create categories for your envelopes.**

   Categories will include areas where overspending of cash may occur between each paycheck if there were no control mechanism. Examples could be food, gas, clothing, and entertainment.

4. Place cash into your envelopes.

After you've determined and categorized your cash expenses, load each envelope with the allotted amount of cash. For example, if you allow $50 for entertainment, put $50 cash in your entertainment envelope for the pay period.

5. When the envelope is empty, you're done spending.

It really is that simple. When you have spent all the cash in any particular envelope, you're finished spending for that category. So be aware, if you have an expensive night on the town and spend your entire $50 on entertainment in one evening, you must discipline yourself not to spend any more on entertainment until your next pay period, when you can budget for that category again.

6. No cheating!

This system will take discipline and time to get used to. Do your best not to simply visit an ATM when you find yourself short on cash in any particular category. Remember, you can always reassess your budget each month and adjust your predetermined allotment ahead of time.

7. Remember, you're a cash person now.

The days of overspending with your debit card are over. Even though the funds used with your debit card came directly from your checking or savings account, this ease of spending causes many to overspend. For most, spending cash is more difficult than swiping plastic. By becoming a cash-only consumer, you'll be less likely to overspend or buy on impulse.

8. **Be patient.**

   Remember, establishing a responsible spending plan is part of your lifestyle, not a passing experiment. Your financial routines may take months or years to perfect. Don't give up after a month or two if you become frustrated. Eventually you'll be more comfortable knowing where and how much you are spending each pay period. Trust me; staying financially stable is something you'll be proud of. If you're patient, you'll see for yourself how exciting living a debt-free lifestyle and building wealth can be!

THE 60% SOLUTION

Another simple budgeting strategy I've found is the 60% solution. With this budget, you structure your regular monthly expenses within 60% of your gross income. This also includes both long- and short-term savings, retirement, and spending money (entertainment, clothing, etc.). These are often considered the items that cause a budget to fail, because most people don't budget for them.

With this technique, you use percentages to determine your monthly spending. Ideally, 60% of your income is set aside for monthly expenses, hence the name. The other 40% can be divided among your retirement account, short- and long-term savings, and entertainment.

For example, multiply the amount of your monthly income by 60%, or 0.60. This is the amount you should spend on things like housing, vehicle expenses, Internet, cable, food, utilities, and other monthly bills. Subtract this amount from the total. The remaining amount can be divided evenly, or however else you choose to divide it, among your retirement account, emergency fund or debt reduction, short-term savings for periodic expenses, and entertainment.

Let's take a look at an example of how this budget strategy may look in real life. Keep in mind that your percentages will vary, and some of the expenses may not even apply if you are currently serving in the military. The following example can be viewed as a guide for educational purposes.

60% MONTHLY EXPENSES

This would include items such as housing, food, utilities, vehicles, insurance, and child care. Most often, these are the costs of living that are most considered when establishing a budget.

10% SHORT-TERM SAVINGS

This savings account is designated for periodic expenses. Examples may include medical expenses, vehicle maintenance or repairs (not including insurance premiums), appliances, home maintenance, and Christmas and birthday gifts. The short-term savings account gives you the confidence that you will have the money for these things as they arise, and, at the same time, you will not overspend beyond your planned budget.

10% LONG-TERM SAVINGS OR DEBT REDUCTION

If you are in debt (not including a home mortgage), it may be wise to use this portion of the budget to pay off your debts, and even draw some from the other categories, such as retirement, to increase this to about 20% for now. After your debt has been paid off, it may be wise to consult a financial advisor regarding a conservative approach to investing these funds, since they are intended for long-term savings. An example could be an index fund due to its liquidity and relatively low risk.

10% RETIREMENT

When setting up retirement funds, strongly consider having these accounts set up for automatic withdrawal. To begin, examples could include a military thrift savings plan or Roth IRA.

10% ENTERTAINMENT

Service members perform some of the most difficult jobs in the world and spend long hours each day doing them. These funds should be set aside for you to enjoy—whatever it is!

FLEXIBILITY IS IMPORTANT WHILE BUDGETING

In the military, fragmentary orders are abbreviated operation orders that are used to adjust or modify the original order. They eliminate the need to restate information and create a whole new order. You can apply this same approach to your budget. From month to month, your lifestyle may change without notice, and you need to adjust your finances along the way.

Marriage or divorce, new babies, deployment orders, unexpected illnesses, and physical injuries are all things that might mean you need to adjust your finances. If you have set up a budget that addresses unexpected costs, you can simply adjust the numbers as needed. This way, you will be ready, willing, and able to do so anytime. Your planning and flexibility ensure your financial stability.

MAINTAIN YOUR PLAN FIFTEEN TO TWENTY MINUTES A WEEK

Please do not assume that your own budget will not require routine maintenance to ensure its accuracy. You should devote fifteen to twenty minutes a week to reviewing your budget and confirming that your finances are in order. Set a day and time when you take a look at your finances each week, and this routine will provide you with peace of mind that you are not overextending your spending.

YOUR OWN BUDGET STRATEGY

The budget and spending plans we've reviewed are fairly simple, and these are only a few of the techniques folks use to organize their spending. The technique that works for you will likely evolve over time. No matter what you try, though, you will quickly gain confidence from knowing that you are taking charge of your financial future.

Chapter 13

A Shared Vision

"Military husband and wife together set their sights on astounding goal"

Petty Officer(s) Cooper
US Navy

One of the greatest examples of financial goal setting was that of Mr. and Mrs. Cooper. They were both in their midtwenties, were happily married, and were both petty officers second class serving in the US Navy.

Together, they had a combined monthly income of nearly $5,000. And because of their ability to save money by living in military housing, Mr. Cooper explained that they rarely spent even half of their monthly paychecks. They simply directed the remaining $2,000–$3000 into a diversified portfolio that consisted primarily of the Thrift Savings Plan (TSP) offered through the military in addition to a few other conservative investments, including a Roth IRA, two index funds, mutual funds, and certificates of deposit. (These investment tools will be defined in later chapters.)

For years they lived a financially conservative lifestyle and focused on enjoying the simple things life offered. Their plan was to both achieve the rank of senior chief petty officer prior to retiring from the Navy. If they succeed in accomplishing their goal, they'll have a significant pension between the two of them in addition to their savings. They may consider other career interests after serving in the US Navy, but they plan to completely retire in their midfifties!

Similar to the story of retired Marine Corps Colonel Walsh in chapter 8, the Coopers deposited a great deal of money into a specific savings account designated for building a new home upon retirement. What a wonderful reward for their years of planning and dedication to their savings plans. According to Mr. Cooper, he attributed their success to their ability to remain focused on their long-term goals. Many times over the years of their career, their foresight allowed them to avoid temptations of squandering their money on luxury items. In addition, their success was ensured by their shared vision of a secure and prosperous financial future.

Chapter 14

Needs Versus Wants

Before you can successfully create and apply a savings and investment plan, you need to learn to determine the difference between your needs and your wants.

The spending habits you develop today will have a significant impact on your financial conditions in the years to come. It will be necessary for you to first determine what is truly important in your life. It is up to you to decide when you will make this decision. Will you do so when you finish reading this book? Or will you decide in your forties, fifties, or sixties, when you are scrambling to save money to make up for the time you have lost? Wouldn't you agree that now is as good a time as any? The life you lead today will directly impact the purchases you consider necessary. As your life evolves, you'll begin to realize something: the more you decide to live without, the happier you will be in the long run.

And this can only happen once you've started to separate your needs from your wants.

WHAT ARE NEEDS?

The first step when breaking free from living beyond your means is to come to a clear understanding of the difference between needs and wants. Each of us has certain needs we require to live our daily lives. Examples of needs include:

- Clean water
- Nutrition
- Medical treatment
- Medication
- Basic transportation
- A safe place to live
- Clothing

WHAT ARE WANTS?

After our basic needs are satisfied, we have other material items and services that we purchase or use. These can be defined as wants. These are things that make our lives more enjoyable, comfortable, and convenient. Wants are certain goods and services we may be able to do without if we have to. Examples of wants include:

- Luxury cars
- Recreational vehicles, such as boats, snowmobiles, and motorcycles

- Second homes
- Home computers
- Laundering service
- High-speed Internet
- Jewelry
- New furniture
- Swimming pools
- Premium TV packages
- Entertainment, like going to the movies or concerts
- Eating out
- Designer clothing

Did you notice that the list of wants could go on and on and on? It is apparent that the majority of us spend more than we can afford on luxury items and services we could possibly do without.

EVERYONE'S NEEDS AND WANTS ARE DIFFERENT

One individual's wants may be another person's needs, and vice versa. For example, a farmer may *need* a full-size four-wheel-drive truck to operate on his farm. On the contrary, a teenager in a large city might *want* the same type of vehicle. However, it is possible to get by with a much more economical vehicle in a large city.

NEEDS ARE CONTINUALLY CHANGING

Throughout our lives, our needs continually change. From the time we are infants to the time we retire, the things we need cannot remain the same. Here are some factors that alter our needs:

- Marriage
- Death in the family
- Having children
- Divorce
- Sudden injury
- Health concerns

PERCEIVED NEEDS OF A NEW GENERATION

Modern society has created a multitude of new goods and services that many people view as requirements. A few examples include:

- Gas-guzzling SUVs
- Cell phones
- Eight-dollar cups of coffee
- Cable TV with 1,300 channels
- Designer clothes
- Computer games

These are just a few of the luxuries considered by many to be modern-day staples. Marketing and advertising campaigns have led us to believe that we are not living life to the fullest without them. As a result, living beyond our incomes has become a common theme that is only promoted by our supersize culture and fueled by addiction to credit cards.

HOW DO I DETERMINE MY OWN NEEDS AND WANTS?

When attempting to significantly decrease your spending, it is necessary to take a critical look at what you consider needs. Every time you find yourself about to purchase something, stop and consider whether it is a need or a want. Doing so is an excellent beginning to a financially responsible lifestyle.

KEEP A RECORD TO MAKE DETERMINATIONS

Before you begin to alter your spending habits, you may find it helpful to keep a record of what you are spending during the course of one month. Try comparing what you spend each month to your monthly income. This will prove to be a valuable tool. With it, you will see exactly how much of your spending is applied toward things you want, but don't necessarily need. Continue to do this for several months as you begin to develop new spending habits.

By continuing to keep a record of your spending habits, it is likely that you will notice a significant decrease over time. If not, you will be able to see exactly where your money is going and where you can make appropriate adjustments if need be. A record of your spending will provide a visual representation of your cash flow, making it much easier to monitor. Once you begin to get organized, you'll be well on your way to living a less expensive and more fulfilling life!

THE "I WANT IT NOW" SOCIETY

I've heard many people say that today's generation attempts to have everything our parents have, but at an age when we can't afford it. In a society where credit is routinely available, who is responsible for this? Is it the borrower or the lender?

Many borrowers undoubtedly use poor judgment. However, in their defense, it may be extremely difficult to say no when lenders are not requiring a single penny for a down payment on a new home available with a balloon loan. Or when vehicles that are well beyond a borrower's means can be financed for up to seven years. Or when countless luxury items are available for purchase with the simple swipe of a credit card.

But borrowers have to remember that not one of the items mentioned actually belongs to them, since they are not paid for yet. And credit card and loan companies are charging outrageous monthly interest on them. Understanding this concept is the borrowers' responsibility.

I WORK HARD—I DESERVE A REWARD!

Men and women from all walks of life often feel that they deserve to be rewarded for the hard work they have performed. For generations, servicemen and servicewomen have rewarded themselves with all sorts of extravagant material items when returning home from deployment to a war zone. With modern combat pay increases and sizable reenlistment bonuses, luxurious rewards for hard work have never seemed more enticing.

Planning to spend a modest portion of your earnings on luxury items upon return from deployment can be a source of motivation while overseas. However, spending every cent you have saved can suddenly turn a motivator into a financial nightmare.

One solution is to focus some of your attention on nontangible rewards, such as:

- The peace of mind you get from having zero debt
- A substantial bank account that is earning interest
- A clear vision of your financially secure future
- The ability to pay a sizable amount of cash toward a new home
- Retirement at an earlier age than you might otherwise anticipate

A simpler lifestyle can benefit you in a number of ways. The confidence you gain from living a financially sound and secure life will help you develop a sense of pride that will last long after any luxury item has diminished in value.

You may find your peers admiring the confidence you exude from your debt-free lifestyle. But mainly, you will find a deeper sense of happiness when you realize that you are getting by without all the expensive things you can't really afford anyway.

Why not consider giving a simpler lifestyle a try? You can always spend the money later if you decide the simple life is not for you. What do you have to lose?

A GREATER APPRECIATION FOR WHAT YOU ALREADY HAVE

Material items Many service members who deploy to developing nations and war zones often acquire a nontangible asset that will prove to be more valuable than any monetary gain. The benefit that I am referring to is an enhanced appreciation for the things you already have in your life and an understanding of the material possessions a person can do without. This elevated level of gratitude for what you already have can dramatically alter your perspective on life. This outlook is nearly unavoidable after returning home from a developing nation besieged by war and plagued by poverty and disease.

Health Dismal images of innocent people struggling to survive will likely change your point of view toward luxurious material items you once considered essential. Hopefully, you will begin to place a superior value on the basics of life, such as your own and your family's health, clean water, food, clothing, and a safe neighborhood to live in.

After seeing hundreds of people unable to attain these basic requirements, the objects you once desired may begin to seem insignificant. This feeling is compounded when you realize that your health could be taken from you at any time. After witnessing, firsthand, unimaginable levels of suffering, it seems impossible not to develop a deeper sense of gratitude for your own health and for the health of those you love.

Freedom Following a deployment to a developing nation, you will likely gain a fuller understanding of what it means to live in a country free of tyranny and in a society based on freedom and civil liberties that are frequently overlooked by many of its very own citizens. After experiencing the condition of good people who are far less fortunate, it seems shameful not to possess a heightened level of appreciation for the blessing of being born in such a privileged nation.

A PRIME EXAMPLE OF NEEDS VS. WANTS

The difference between purchasing a quality preowned vehicle and a new vehicle can greatly affect your long-term savings plan. I purchased my first brand-new vehicle when I was only eighteen, for $17,000. For argument's sake, we'll say I could have purchased a quality preowned vehicle for $7,000, leaving $10,000 available to invest at my discretion. Let's also say that I set a goal to retire at the age of fifty-eight. This would have left forty years for the $10,000 to grow due to the compound interest. If the $10,000 had been placed in a conservative index fund that earned 4% annually, it could have possibly grown to nearly $50,000 by the time I retired. If I had decided to leave the fund alone for another twenty years, feasibly it could have grown to $100,000.

WOULD YOU RATHER PAY YOUR DUES NOW OR IN YOUR GOLDEN YEARS?

As far as motivation goes, you might try considering the financial sacrifices you make today as a way of "paying your dues" for a promising financial future tomorrow. At one point or another, we all have to pay our financial dues. So why not do it now, while you are young and healthy? It's easier to get by with less today than it will be later in life. Once you are moving toward a financially secure future, your motivation will increase because you will have a prosperous future to look forward to.

If you choose to pay your dues now by not spending your money on unnecessary material items or services that only serve to make your life more convenient, your portfolio has the potential to grow at a tremendously greater rate. If you choose to pay your dues later by spending unnecessarily today, you will work harder for less money during the years when you could be enjoying life the most.

GOOD NEWS FOR THE NEXT GENERATION

My hope is that future generations will be taught more conservative spending habits and that they will learn lessons about the pitfalls of accumulating debt by observing the spending habits of today's consumers. If this were to happen, young people might not only benefit financially, but also discover that true satisfaction in life comes from faith, family, friendship, and helping others.

Chapter 15

Simple Can Be Effective

"By age sixty-five, my principle investment will grow to nearly $100,000."

Staff Sergeant Fritz
US Army $10 a day

Staff Sergeant Fritz explained that when he first enlisted, he spent every cent of his hard-earned pay. After completing his first year in the military, he realized that he had nothing to show for his time and effort, so he decided to make a change. He wanted to save a portion of his pay, but he just wasn't sure where to begin. So five years ago he simply began saving $10 every day.

Today, the financial institution where Staff Sergeant Fritz invested his money projects his account could grow to nearly $100,000 by age sixty-five. This is without adding an additional cent.

HOW IS THIS POSSIBLE ON $10 A DAY?

Staff Sergeant Fritz designated $10 a day to be placed into a relatively conservative mutual fund at the end of every month. He consistently deposited the $300 every month for five years while earning an average 4% interest. Currently, the account balance is nearing $20,000. Now all Staff Sergeant Fritz has to do is leave the balance in the account and continue benefiting from the accumulating interest. By the time he's sixty-five, his principle investment will have grown to nearly $100,000. Better yet, if he decides to continue stashing $10 a day into the account, the balance has the potential to grow to over $400,000. If nothing else, Staff Sergeant Fritz's savings plan proves one thing: simple can be effective.

Chapter 16

Where Do I Begin Investing?

AN OVERWHELMING TASK?

Designing a lifelong structured investment plan can seem pretty overwhelming. For many, the most difficult part is just getting started. Once you've mastered the basics, though—and hopefully this book will help with that—you will discover that an effective investment portfolio isn't so challenging after all. It's merely a matter of simple arithmetic.

A BASIC SAVINGS ACCOUNT IS A GREAT PLACE TO START!

Although it might seem simple, a basic savings account is one of the most beneficial tools for creating the foundation for your successful financial plan. A savings account can help you manage your financial goals and earn interest at the same time.

BENEFITS OF A SAVINGS ACCOUNT:

- Federal Deposit Insurance Corporation (FDIC) insured; the FDIC is a federal agency that currently insures deposits in member banks and thrifts up to $250,000
- It is a convenient place to store your money
- Interest earned can boost your savings
- Allows you to purchase items with cash rather than borrowing money
- Helps you meet your goals sooner than if you saved your money at home

START EARLY

You have learned that you have an enormous advantage over your civilian counterparts if you begin saving immediately. When others have not even begun to think about a savings plan, you can be well on your way to securing your financial future. By starting to save early, you will need to make fewer financial adjustments in your lifestyle down the road.

For example, if you accumulated $4,000 in savings after completing basic training and placed it in an account that earned 4% interest, and didn't touch it for fifty years, you'd have nearly $30,000. And if you decided to add an additional $200 per month for all those years, your account could potentially grow to over $400,000. Not too bad for such a simple plan.

Like many challenges in life, the most difficult part of securing your finances is getting started. Where do you begin?

WALK BEFORE YOU RUN

As I am sure you have figured out, the commitment to achieve your financial goals does not end in a few years—it is a commitment that lasts a lifetime. It will be much easier for you to start by taking small steps toward your goal and adding new steps as the old ones become second nature. It's just like improving your running ability in basic training; you begin with one mile and slowly increase your speed and mileage as you improve over time.

CONSIDER OPENING MULTIPLE SAVINGS ACCOUNTS

Having more than one savings account allows you to designate funds for specific goals. By designating portions of your income to a specific account, you can track their status at a glance.

Let's consider three savings accounts:

First savings account

This is your emergency expense account. These savings are for emergencies only. Examples are the loss of a job, unanticipated medical expenses from an illness or injury, death in the family, etc.

Second savings account

This account should be for larger expenses and purchases in the long term. Examples are furniture, home maintenance and improvements, vehicle maintenance and repairs, vacations, etc.

Third savings account

This is your retirement savings account. This account gives you the ability to store funds after maxing out an IRA. Because you may withdraw funds without penalty from this account, you can still use portions of these savings and apply them to a diversity of investments. Examples are certificates of deposit, Roth IRAs, mutual funds, etc.

EMERGENCY FUND SAVINGS ACCOUNT

Before you begin paying off debts, it is vital that you have at least a small emergency fund established. An emergency savings account is fundamental for a healthy financial plan to succeed. Without a cushion of money to absorb the costs of unforeseen expenses, such situations can leave you financially devastated. Your emergency money will prevent a time of emergency from becoming a financial crisis. You can start today by designating a savings account specifically for emergencies.

HOW MUCH MONEY SHOULD YOU HAVE IN YOUR EMERGENCY ACCOUNT?

To begin, set an attainable goal of $1,000. You can add to it as you improve the accuracy of your budget. Many might agree that an individual's ideal target amount for an emergency fund would be three to six months of living expenses. This amount should be sufficient for most emergency expenses as they arise.

FUNDING YOUR EMERGENCY ACCOUNT

On a budget that's already spread thin, funding your emergency account can be a challenging task. This may be why the average consumer does not have an emergency fund account. However difficult, you should consider making it a priority.

Some people treat their emergency fund as if it were a mandatory monthly bill. They pay into their emergency fund account each month as if they were paying their electric or gas bill. In this way, even if funds are withdrawn, they are already beginning to be replaced the following month.

Others place a large amount of money all at once into the account, say, from a tax return or reenlistment bonus. However you can manage it, make sure you set aside emergency funds. I cannot stress how important this is in maintaining your financial security and helping you avoid going into debt.

WHERE SHOULD I STORE MY EMERGENCY FUNDS?

Some likely options could be placing your savings in a money market account or a savings account. Money markets and savings accounts can both be places to park your funds until they are needed. They both have low risk and excellent liquidity factors.

Personally, I use a savings account and a money market account. The money market account has a slightly higher interest rate and is slightly less accessible, so there is less chance that I will spend the money on nonemergency expenses.

When I have three months' worth of living expenses in my savings account, I move one month's worth of expenses into the money market account. I continue to save money in my savings account until I can place one month's expenses into the money market account. That way, I have some emergency funds available all the time and the peace of mind that more could be available from the money market account if necessary.

The technique I have just described is an old one and can prove to be very effective when you are attempting to maximize the earning potential of your emergency savings. However, there is no reason that you need to make your own plan this complex. Simply saving up six months' worth of living expenses in a regular savings account is a perfect way to begin. The main idea is to consistently replenish any funds that are withdrawn and use the money only when you are facing a real emergency.

WHAT IS A MONEY MARKET ACCOUNT?

A money market account is a financial account that pays interest based on current interest rates. Typically, money market accounts have higher rates of return than traditional savings accounts, but the account limits how many withdrawals you are allowed per month. A money market account may also require a minimum balance, anywhere from $1,000 to $25,000 to earn interest or avoid costly fees. If a money market account is utilized as an emergency fund, these criteria may not be all bad since they deter the owner from making hasty withdrawals.

REMEMBER, USE EMERGENCY FUNDS ONLY FOR EMERGENCIES!

Once you have established an emergency account, you may find the money it contains to be an extraordinary temptation. You must remind yourself that the name of the account says it all—emergency funds. You need to develop the willpower to honestly assess what constitutes an emergency and what does not.

It also may be tempting to use these designated funds to pay off existing debt, and understandably so. However, if you do this and then find yourself facing an emergency, you may end up using credit and end up right back where you started. A better idea is to fund your emergency account and then forget that it exists.

ADJUSTING YOUR FUNDING

Beginning a savings plan can be difficult for all of us. In order to ease the pain while you are changing your spending habits, it is important to keep in mind that you can adjust your plan at any time.

For instance, suppose that after you save everything you can for three months, you find it necessary to dip into your emergency savings fund to make ends meet. If this is the case, the amount you were saving was probably a bit too much. Use only what you need in order to get by, and then adjust your plan so that you are still saving consistently, but just a little less each month.

On the other hand, there might be times in your life that you can increase your savings; for example, if you receive a pay raise, promotion, tax return, or reenlistment bonus. And again, at other times you may need to decrease your savings—for instance, if you find yourself with a new baby, involved in a divorce, or afflicted with a sudden injury or illness. As life continues on, you'll begin to realize your finances continually need adjusting.

DIFFERENT PEOPLE HAVE DIFFERENT NEEDS

At this point, you might be thinking that you understand the message of this book and why it so beneficial to save, especially while you're young. But maybe your goals are a little less lofty. Perhaps you are thinking that you don't need to have a million dollars. Or maybe you're not planning on staying in the military for thirty years. Not a problem. You don't have to follow the specifics that are outlined here in order to follow the general theme. You can adjust your savings plan accordingly. Determine what your needs and wants are and how much you will need to secure your lifestyle during retirement, and then use the principles you have learned here to help you reach your goals.

TIPS FOR SELECTING A SAVINGS ACCOUNT

CONFIRM THE ACCESSIBILITY OF YOUR DEPOSITS.

Every bank has its own guidelines for depositing funds into and withdrawing funds from a savings account. If you intend to use an ATM regularly, find out what fees are associated with the process at the financial institution.

CHECK FOR MONTHLY MAINTENANCE FEES.

Some banks routinely charge fees for things like processing your transactions, withdrawing money, and even transferring funds from one account to another. If your financial institution charges such fees, you would be wise to shop around. Competition can be fierce among financial institutions, and it is likely that you will find one with free savings and checking accounts.

FIND A DECENT INTEREST RATE.

Every bank is different, so if you find more than one institution with free accounts, check the interest rates offered. Choose the one that pays you most for doing business with it.

LOOK INTO MINIMUM BALANCE REQUIREMENTS.

Some banks actually charge a fee if your balance falls below its selected minimum balance. Reconsider using a bank that has minimum balance requirements. It can be frustrating to withdraw money because you are facing a financial emergency and then find yourself penalized for using your own money. Shop around to find a bank that does not practice such a policy.

YOU'RE NOT THE ONLY ONE

At times, it might seem like you are the only one who has ever struggled to save money. This definitely is not true. Even people with the most frugal of lifestyles often become overwhelmed by the difficulty of saving money. But when you realize that you don't even miss the things you are getting by without, investing your money will become even more rewarding. When your savings plan is established and the money in your accounts begins to grow more rapidly, your thrifty spending habits will become easier and easier.

By reading this book and learning how to plan for a financially sound future, you are well ahead of others who may not ever gain this information. Give your plan time to develop and mature. You will be extremely proud of yourself when it does.

A REMARKABLE START

Take a second now to pat yourself on the back. By simply reading the first several chapters of this book, you have done far more for yourself, financially, than the average person your age. Congratulations!

Chapter 17

Conquering a Mountain

"We managed to pay off $45,000 in debt in just three years."

Private First Class Allen
US Army

Private First Class Allen had just completed basic training, and he and his fiancé had recently arrived in our unit. He was assigned to the mortar team in our platoon. It seemed like he was always optimistic, full of energy, and lived for his job. You may know the type. All of which added to my surprise when he told me how far in debt he was.

He explained to me that three years ago he had first been approved for a credit card. He was only eighteen years old at the time. The card had an interest rate of 12% and a $500 credit limit. That was only the beginning. Just three years after graduating from high school, he'd accumulated nearly $10,000 in debt between five different credit card companies. Recently, in anticipation of his enlistment bonus and the certainty of a steady income from his military pay, he had financed a brand-new vehicle rather than paying down his debt.

Private First Class Allen and his fiancée now owed nearly $45,000 to lenders, and had just found out they were expecting a baby. They were able to make only the minimum payments on their credit cards because of their careless spending habits. This included the latest electronics, designer clothing, and frequent evenings out in upscale restaurants. There was absolutely nothing left for savings at the end of each month. To say the Allens were overwhelmed by their financial situation was an understatement.

That conversation took place over four years ago. Recently, I spoke to Private First Class Allen on the phone, and he told me that he and his wife had totally turned their finances around. They had completely overhauled their budget and their frivolous spending habits. After reorganizing their finances, they were able to pay off all of their debt, even their vehicles. Now, anything they don't have cash for, they realize they cannot afford. Both have joined the National Guard, and in the fall they will both be attending college, with their sights set on lucrative careers that they are excited about.

The Allens were fortunate to have the foresight and determination to make these financial changes while they were young. Overcoming their mountain of debt would not have been possible without their willingness to change.

CHAPTER 18

ELIMINATING DEBT...IT'S AN UPHILL BATTLE

If this chapter does not apply to you, congratulations! With no debt to pay down, you are well ahead of the average American citizen in regards to saving for your future. To state the obvious, having no debts to pay is an enormous advantage and will allow you to accelerate your savings and investment plans.

However, if you are similar to the majority of Americans, you probably have some type of financial obligations. Perhaps credit cards, student loans, vehicle loans? You may be struggling with your monthly expenses and searching for options to get a handle on your credit obligations. If you have found yourself doing things like paying monthly bills with your credit card, it is likely you will eventually have serious financial problems that may result in bankruptcy.

For those who were allowed to overextend their spending by unscrupulous lending institutions that provided credit they shouldn't have and are now charging excessive interest rates and fees, getting out of debt can be more of a challenging task than anticipated. How much cash do you think the average person has to spend each year just to pay interest on credit card debt or home loans, car loans or student loans? It's obscene. There is no reason to live that way. None.

ELIMINATING DEBT FIRST

Mathematically, it doesn't make sense for an investor to deposit $5,000 into a mutual fund anticipating a 4% return if he or she owes $10,000 in credit card debt with a 12% interest rate. Thus, before you begin a serious investment plan, a better option would be to eliminate all of your debts, with the exception of a home mortgage. Ideally, becoming debt free first should be your primary goal. In other words, when you begin investing, you'll need to do so with a clean slate. This strategy not only makes mathematical sense, but it will also give you a new sense of respect for good spending habits when you see how difficult it can be to pay off the debts you currently owe.

A MATHEMATICAL EXAMPLE

This example will show you the astronomical amount of money you can save by paying off your credit cards as quickly as possible. Assume that the owner of this card has stopped using it and is merely paying off debt he or she has already accumulated.

Credit Card Debt	Monthly Payment	Interest Rate	Months to Pay Off Debt	Estimated Total Interest Accrued
$20,000.00	$264.30	10%	120	$11,716.18
$20,000.00	$424.94	10%	60	$5,496.45
Savings				$6,219.73

By choosing to pay off credit card debt in five years rather than ten, you can save more than $6,000!

When paying only the minimum amount owed on a credit card each month, it is possible to pay more in interest than the cost of your original purchase. If you increase your monthly payment by even the slightest amount, you will dramatically cut down the time it takes to pay off your debt in addition to the total interest paid. As you can see, purchasing a little less and reducing your debt a little more can make a tremendous difference!

WHERE TO BEGIN?

After determining how much of your monthly budget you will use to pay off debt, you need to form a strategy for doing so. This is not an exact science. Some prefer to set a goal of paying off the credit cards with the highest interest first. Others pay off debts with the smallest balances first to simplify their monthly obligations and see fast results. This method can be a significant motivator. Explore different methods for yourself, find what works best for you, and stick with it!

DEBT CONSOLIDATION

If you owe money to more than one credit card company, you may choose to use debt consolidation. This technique consists of transferring the balance on high interest cards to lower interest cards and then canceling the card with high interest rates. It can save you money in interest and also save you the labor of paying so many bills per month, which lessens the possibility of missed payments and late fees.

Caution: if you consider debt consolidation, use extreme discretion when doing so. Thoroughly research any possible adverse effects, such as transfer fees and penalties hidden in a company's guidelines. It is important to remember that these companies make money by offering you such low monthly payments. They may not perceive paying off your credit balance as a good thing, and may even penalize you for doing so.

THE SNOWBALL EFFECT

The snowball effect can be a tremendous motivator when it comes to challenging yourself to live within your means. This strategy is based on the fact that while you are paying extra on one credit card, you must still make the minimum payments on your others. So, when you are finished paying off a card, simply apply the amount you were paying on it each month to another credit card, in addition to the minimum payment you were making. Each debt you pay off will take less time than the last one did.

ACCELERATE YOUR DEBT PAYMENT

Are you anticipating a sizable tax refund or reenlistment bonus? These can be excellent accelerators in debt reduction if you plan ahead. Simply use the money to blast away credit card debt or a car loan. Plan ahead, earmark the additional funds in advance, and then just pretend you never received them. Chances are you won't even miss the extra income. You will gain the money back in short order through the interest you will not have to pay.

BECOME A CASH-ONLY PERSON

Here's an original thought: if you cannot pay cash for a purchase, you can't afford it! This concept seems to be a thing of the past because of the availability of unrealistically high credit limits offered by questionable lending institutions. With the possible exception of your home, why would you not just spend cash on a purchase? It is a simple concept that requires nothing but discipline and patience. Save up your money while earning interest on it—and then buy with cash!

PURCHASE YOUR NEXT VEHICLE WITH CASH

Yes, contrary to popular belief, people do still pay cash for vehicles. How? Start small. If you shop around, you can find plenty of reliable vehicles that are for sale by their owners at affordable prices. After purchasing a reliable vehicle with cash, you can continue to save to upgrade your vehicle in the future—again with cash.

Saving your money to pay cash for a vehicle can be extremely gratifying. While saving, shop around on the Internet and in your local area for a vehicle you can afford. When you find one that appears to be clean and mechanically sound, make an offer that is less than the asking price, and pay for it with cash. That's it. You will save on your monthly insurance bill and have no monthly payment to boot.

Over the years, you can upgrade in make and model with your accumulated savings. After you upgrade your vehicle, you can sell the old one and deposit that money back into your savings plan. By starting small and paying cash, you can avoid outrageous interest rates, dealership costs, and sales fees. In the long term, you'll enjoy lower insurance rates as well.

DON'T USE YOUR EMERGENCY ACCOUNT TO PAY OFF YOUR DEBT

Now that you have established your emergency account, you may be tempted to use it to pay down your debt. Don't. Paying off debt as soon as possible is extremely important; however, you should not use your emergency account to do so.

The purpose of the emergency account is to cover expenses if and when emergencies arise. By exhausting this vital resource, you may end up further in debt when you're forced to use credit to handle true unexpected emergency expenses. Pretend the emergency fund doesn't even exist, unless you are facing a real emergency.

CREDIT CARDS

As you can see in the following graph, average American credit card debt has increased to an unacceptable level since 1990. Today, many credit card companies are owned by foreign banks. Overextended financial debt due to the misuse of credit cards has committed billions of US dollars to foreign investors.

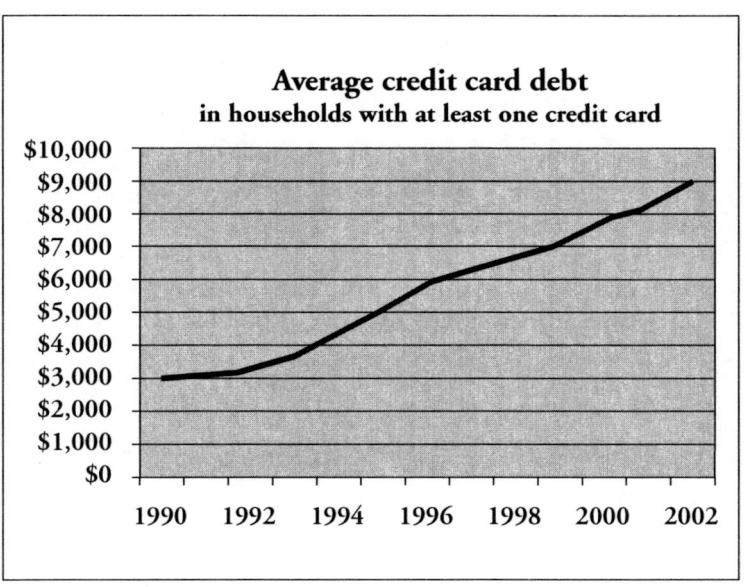

TEN REASONS NOT TO USE CREDIT CARDS

Believe it or not, some folks say they love using their credit cards for all of their purchases. In my opinion, the dangers of using credit cards easily outweigh their convenience.

The following are ten simplified reasons not to routinely use credit cards:

1. The average consumer may have a tendency to spend more with credit cards than with cash.
2. Using credit cards, rather than cash, may increase the risk of identity theft.
3. Credit cards may cause the consumer to fall behind on monthly bills.
4. Tracking and paying credit card bills is more work than strictly paying cash.
5. Credit card companies generally charge a higher interest rate than conventional lenders.
6. Credit cards subject the consumer to outlandish penalties and fees.
7. Rewards promoted by credit card lenders are a trick to get consumers to use their card more.
8. Credit cards may increase a person's tendency to purchase impulsively.
9. Credit cards simply create another monthly bill a person is responsible for paying.
10. Overextending credit to a population may exacerbate a financial recession.

If you are smart, this list should convince you that overusing credit cards for daily spending is not a good idea. Wise up now! Cancel your credit cards, and cut them up today. You will be glad you did tomorrow.

WHAT IS IMPULSE PURCHASING?

Impulse buying occurs when a consumer gets caught up in the excitement of a situation and purchases something without giving it enough consideration. It generally means buying something you don't really need or even want. Sale signs stating "50% off, today only!" are retailers' attempts to provoke impulse buying. To prevent yourself from giving in to such temptation, you need to slow down and take time to consider all of your purchases.

HOW DO I AVOID AN IMPULSIVE PURCHASE?

The answer is time. A simple technique is just to walk away from the item in question and give it time. For larger-ticket items, give yourself a month to think about it. If you still feel like you need the item after that, you're probably right.

DO CREDIT CARDS INCREASE IMPULSE PURCHASING?

A person that routinely spends impulsively and credit cards are a volatile combination. The purchase of an item you don't need, with money you don't have, is a disaster right from the beginning. These spending practices are the catalyst that will propel you into a financial scenario that unfortunately may end in bankruptcy.

Save your money first, and pay cash for everything. You may even find that by the time you save the money for something, you don't want or need the item anymore. Once you start, you may find it more difficult to hand over your cash than to swipe a credit card. Remember, if you don't have cash for something, you can't afford it. It's as simple as that.

KEEPING UP WITH THE MODERN-DAY JONESES

Professional athletes, dim-witted celebrities, and rock stars paid multimillions have escalated the expression "keeping up with the Joneses." Their flamboyant, wasteful behavior is shoved in the face of the working class. Is it possible this could affect how young people spend their money? Absolutely. Many try to emulate the lifestyles of their "heroes" without a full understanding of the true cost, and, while doing so, oftentimes max out numerous sources of credit.

When you are creating your own financial plan, consider a comfortable but conservative lifestyle. Be realistic. Set quality long-term goals for your future, rather than raising the bar too high just to keep up with the modern-day Joneses.

NEVER GIVE UP

One thing I recommend to those who are struggling with their finances and debt reduction is to look online for financial advice blogs. You will quickly realize that there are countless others out there just like you, struggling with the same type of concerns. By interacting with others whose stories are similar to your own, you just might come across some additional ideas that will work for you.

JUST DO IT!

The bottom line is that you need to make a plan to reduce your debt today. A good plan today is better than a perfect plan tomorrow. And no matter how you do it, becoming debt free will have the same result: a life free of financial anxiety, and a secure future.

CHAPTER 19

START SMALL AND GROW BIG

"Savings bonds were a simple way to begin an investment plan."

Major Caroline Levitt
US Air Force

The following is an inspiring story from an Air Force staff sergeant. She explains how her family shared their financial values with the next generation.

My name is Judy Levitt and I am currently a staff sergeant in the US Air Force. Five years ago, I was twenty years old and decided to join the military like my aunt Caroline did in 1981. Aunt Caroline had successfully retired from the Air Force in 2003 as a major after twenty-two years of service. Afterwards, she and my uncle were financially secure enough to work part time doing something they loved: breeding thoroughbred horses on their Montana farm.

During my aunt Caroline's basic training, she was educated on the benefits of investing in savings bonds. She was aware bonds typically yield a lower return than other investments, but they were an extremely secure source to place her hard-earned pay. The security of the bonds and the peace of mind of the low risk involved are what appealed to her most.

After arriving at her first duty station, she began purchasing $50 savings bonds. Throughout her enlistment, she increased the amount of savings bonds she purchased based on the amount of increased pay she received.

"Savings bonds were a simple way to begin an investment plan," she explained. At twenty years old, without any debt, Aunt Caroline was off to a great start.

She described that a great deal of her financial success was attributed to starting good spending habits early in her career. She explained that in the mid-1980s she was fortunate not to be exposed to the availability of credit cards. "Credit cards were not as prevalent as they are today," she advised.

She told me that it was not always easy to dedicate a portion of her pay to her investments. It took discipline, especially at the beginning. However, as time went by and her pay increased, she also began to see her savings increase tremendously. This became a significant motivating factor.

Although Aunt Caroline was successful with numerous additional investments throughout her career, she considered savings bonds to be her bread-and-butter investment and an excellent way to begin investing.

"Without starting with the basics, like I did with bonds, I may not have been motivated to learn about other financial tools. Start small, and you'll grow big," was Aunt Caroline's philosophy. Her story inspired me, and now I hope my story inspires you.

Chapter 20

Types of Investments

The options for investing your money are continually increasing. In this chapter, we'll define numerous possibilities of where to begin placing a portion of your income for your future. Start slowly, and learn as you go. While investing, you must be consistent and stick with your plan.

Before you begin to invest your money, you should first understand your expectations and decide which investment options are suitable for you and your needs. The type of investment depends on the need and time horizon you anticipate. If you want to invest for retirement, there will be different investment options. Numerous investment options will be defined in the chapter. After learning the definitions, plan to speak to a professional financial planner prior to making any monetary commitments. Keep in mind, to lower your risk exposure, it is wise to invest in different investment instruments and make a diversified portfolio.

LET'S TAKE A LOOK AT SOME FINANCIAL SERVICES OFFERED THROUGH THE MILITARY:

THE MILITARY PENSION

A pension is defined as a steady income issued to a person, typically after retirement or if one becomes disabled. Payments are generally made in the form of a guaranteed annuity. There are few private-sector employers that still offer retirement pensions. But some government institutions, such as the military, offer pensions. Currently, to qualify to receive a retirement pension from the military, you must serve for at least twenty years. After that, you'll have the option of staying in the military or retiring, based on your annual pay and variables such as time spent in the service and rank upon honorable discharge.

The military pension plan is outstanding, but will it be enough to fulfill your needs upon retirement? Whatever your answer, there is no doubt that a well-diversified investment portfolio can certainly help.

THE THRIFT SAVINGS PLAN (TSP)

Typically, the thrift savings plan is the simplest way to begin investing. It is an extremely beneficial way for a member of the military to begin an investment plan. Sponsored by the federal government, the TSP is a retirement and savings plan with the purpose of providing retirement income to service members. The fees involved are minuscule in comparison to other investment firms. At the time this edition of *Military Millionaires* was published, a member of the US military was allowed to contribute up to $16,500 annually, compared to only $5,500 for an IRA. The TSP is an excellent tool to begin your investment strategy. For more information, visit your unit's finance department.

THE THRIFT SAVINGS PLAN LIFE CYCLE FUND (TSP "L" FUND)
Thrift Savings Plans now offer "Life Cycle Funds" to those interested in saving for retirement. A Life Cycle Fund typically diversifies your investments based on your target retirement date. The farther away the determined date is, the more risks that may be taken, and vice versa. As you get closer to your target retirement date, your Life Cycle Fund investments become more conservative while still providing the highest possible rate of return. The best part about the TSP Life Cycle Fund is that you do not need to make any of these difficult decisions yourself. They are made by professional fund managers whose only job is to make the most of your money based on your age and projected date of retirement. The TSP "L" Fund is an excellent tool to begin your investment strategy. For more information, visit your unit's finance department.

THE SAVINGS DEPOSIT PROGRAM (SDP)
The military's Savings Deposit Program was first established during the Vietnam era. At the time this book was written, the SDP enabled service members serving

in designated combat zones to earn 10% interest per year on a maximum investment of $10,000. Interest stops accruing ninety days after you leave the combat zone. The SDP is an excellent, guaranteed investment opportunity that allows all deployed service members to earn a fixed interest rate higher than that of any other comparable investment. If applicable, the SDP is an excellent tool to begin your investment strategy. For more information, visit your unit's finance department.

OTHER TYPES OF INVESTMENTS AVAILABLE PUBLICLY

It may seem that there are countless investment opportunities and strategies available in the public sector. So how do you know which are right for you? This question can best be answered through a discussion with your financial planner. However, you may have more confidence in your planner if you have a basic understanding of investing terms and tools beforehand.

The following information will provide an understanding of basic investments. However, you are strongly encouraged to seek professional advice from a financial planner before you begin your investment plan. These definitions are meant to be used only as a guide so that you are more comfortable with the investment opportunities your financial planner may offer you.

Savings accounts

Savings accounts are accounts maintained by retail financial institutions (banks or credit unions) that return a specified interest rate on your deposited funds. A savings account can provide the essential framework for your investment plans while earning interest, and insures your deposits up to $250,000.

In part, a savings account is the easiest and safest way to begin earning interest on your hard-earned military pay. The savings account is a simple tool and a solid foundation for your long-term financial plan. Once placed in a savings account, your money immediately goes to work for you.

CHECKING ACCOUNTS

A checking account is a deposit account at a financial institution into which you can deposit funds for the purpose of security. In addition, you can write checks, withdraw money from an ATM, and make purchases with debit cards.

When opening a checking account, be sure that it is FDIC insured, that you have unlimited withdrawals with no fees, and that you have ATM access, a competitive interest rate, and no minimum balance requirements or fees.

WHEN OPENING A SAVINGS AND/OR A CHECKING ACCOUNT, PLEASE CONSIDER THE FOLLOWING:

- That it is FDIC-insured
- Has unlimited withdrawals with no fees
- ATM access
- A competitive interest rate

- No minimum balance requirements
- No fees if the savings balance falls below a designated amount

CERTIFICATES OF DEPOSIT (CDs)

A CD is a promissory note from a financial institution designed as a time deposit that restricts the holder from withdrawing funds on demand. It is a relatively low-risk instrument that yields a moderate annual percentage rate. Banks and credit unions use the money generated from CDs to fund their investments. In return, they pay interest to you since they are borrowing your money. In essence, the banks pay you one interest rate and then charge the person borrowing money from them a higher interest rate. In the end, both you and the financial institution earn a profit. Your reward for giving up the convenience of withdrawing your money whenever you like is the higher interest rate that you earn compared to, for example, a savings account.

CDs are offered with various lengths of time until their maturity. Maturity dates typically range from three months to seven years. If need be, you can probably withdraw your money before the CD matures, but will be charged a fee for doing so.

If you purchase a one-year CD for $10,000 with an interest rate of 1.8%, it would earn about $180. After one year, you would have $10,180.

A few of the advantages of CDs:

- Low investment risk
- Offer a higher rate of return than a standard savings account

- Initial investments and interest earned are protected up to $250,000 by the FDIC
- Short- to medium-term investments, so they offer earnings sooner than long-term investments
- Typically no fees are required to purchase CDs
- The peace of mind of financial security that you cannot get from stock-market-based investments

A few of the disadvantages of CDs:

- The interest rate is locked in until the maturity date, so if interest rates go up, the rate on your CD will remain the same.
- CD's are subject to all applicable taxes at the local, state, and federal levels.
- There can be steep penalties for withdrawing funds early.
- CDs may be "callable," which means that while you cannot withdraw your money early without penalty, the financial institution can possibly call back your CD before the term ends.
- Interest may not start accruing until the beginning of the month or quarter after you open your CD.

BONDS

Bonds are sold by federal, state, and local governments, public utilities companies, and other institutions in an effort to raise capital through borrowing. Basically, the issuer of the bond promises to pay your money back, with interest, on a specified maturity date. Payments received from a discount bond are paid at the date of maturity. A coupon bond pays a specific amount at the date of maturity in addition to providing a fixed payment over a specified period of time. A good example is a US Treasury bond, which is probably the safest unsecured bond because of the limited risk of default by the issuer.

IRA (INDIVIDUAL RETIREMENT ACCOUNT)

An IRA is a retirement plan that provides some tax advantages. The funds placed in the IRA are not initially taxed, and all income earned is not taxed until withdrawn at retirement.

After funds have been placed in an IRA, the owner of the account advises the director of the financial institution of his or her choice of investments. An IRA owner may select from many types of investments and financial tools. Some institutions do, however, limit your choices to traditional brokerage accounts such as stocks, bonds, and mutual funds.

Funds can be withdrawn at any time, but penalties may be involved for early withdrawal. Taxes will be due for the amount withdrawn during each tax year. The exception is that funds can be withdrawn as taxable income at any time after the age of fifty-nine-and-a-half (retirement age as defined in the terms of an IRA) without penalty.

ROTH IRA

In a Roth IRA, you pay your taxes on the front end, on the money you invest as it is deposited into your account.

Thereafter, your deposited money and interest accumulates tax free. Once you reach retirement age (again, fifty-nine-and-a-half), you can withdraw money from the account as an income source, and any withdrawals are tax free.

When you initially begin investing, you may not consider the advantages of tax strategies. Instead, you will most likely focus on making your money grow. This example will show you the long-term tax advantage of a Roth IRA.

Let's say you establish a Roth IRA with $1,000 when you enlist in the military at age eighteen. You pay about 25% in taxes up front, so only $750 is actually invested. By the time you retire at age sixty-five, that $750 has the potential to grow to approximately $5,000. When you withdraw that money, you receive every penny and pay no additional taxes.

In comparison, if you had invested in a mutual fund that earned the same amount instead, the taxes would apply to the money at the time of withdrawal. If you pay 25% of $1,000 on the front end, it's only $250. But if you pay 25% of $5,000, you're looking at $1,250, so the fund would yield only $3,750.

If you invested the maximum amount in a Roth IRA every year from the age of eighteen until the age of sixty, $5,000.00 per year with a 4% APR, the account balance would be about $544,258.39. Not too bad, eh? The best part is that every penny of that half a million is yours, since you already paid the taxes on it years ago. Investing in a Roth IRA is one of the simplest and smartest investment moves a young person can make.

DEFERRED INCOME

A deferred income plan is an investment option that allows an employee to save for retirement while deferring payment of taxes on both annual income and investment earnings on the amount placed in the fund until withdrawal. Often, larger companies will match a percentage of your contributions. Investors choose the investments they want their deferred income funds invested into; often, stock in the company they work for is one of their options. These deferred income plans may include an employer's matching funds and are referred to by IRS tax code numbers, such as 401(k), 457, and 403b.

MUTUAL FUNDS

Mutual funds pool their investors' funds into a larger fund overseen by a team of professional investment managers. This fund is then invested into a portfolio of various assets or combinations of assets. It may include investment in stocks, bonds, options, futures, currencies, treasuries, and money market securities.

The main concept of a mutual fund is diversification. Your money is spread out across many types of investments, so there is a chance that if one investment is down, another is up. There is less chance of losing money in a mutual fund because diversification lessens the risk of loss.

Mutual funds vary in content and risk. Information regarding the plethora of mutual funds available can be discussed further with your financial advisor. At the time this edition was printed, there were more than ten thousand mutual funds available in North America. No matter what type of investor you are, there is bound to be a mutual fund that fits your style.

STOCKS

A stock may also be known as a share or equity. Basically, a share of stock is a percentage of ownership of a company or corporation. For example, if a company issued one million shares of stock, then ten thousand shares would represent 1% ownership. This ownership gives the owners of the stock the opportunity to benefit from a corporation's profits.

If the price of shares of stock in a company you hold shares in goes up, you make money. This typically happens if a company is earning profits or if speculators anticipate that a company will do well in the future. On the other hand, if a company shows a loss of profits, then you, as a shareholder, may lose money.

INDEX EXCHANGE TRADED FUND (ETF)

An index ETF consists of shares of stock from several companies categorized within a specific market index. It is a fund that attempts to imitate a particular stock index of an individual financial market. Most ETFs attempt to equal the stock market but not outperform it. In other words, the goal of an ETF is to match the returns of a specific stock index, such as the S&P 500 or Dow Jones.

ETFs are not always 100 percent accurate when it comes to mirroring a market, but at times have been known to outperform the markets they are attempting to mirror. If you are just beginning to invest, ETFs can be a safe and lucrative avenue of approach.

SPEAK TO A FINANCIAL ADVISOR

Remember, the preceding information only defines the financial instruments. It was intended to be educational and to assist with your understanding of the diversity of investment tools. It is important to direct any questions you have to your professional financial advisor and consult with an expert before making any decisions involving investments.

With so many variables in investing, even a single conversation with a financial advisor may be helpful.

CHAPTER 21

How Much Should I Invest?

"PAY YOURSELF FIRST"

In the world of personal finance and investing, "paying yourself first" has become a common phrase. Defined, it means prioritizing your investment plan over all other spending. In other words, invest in your future prior to any other expenses. This is accomplished by routing a specified amount of money from each paycheck directly into your investment plan. Consequently, you are paying yourself first.

When applying this concept to your monthly budget, the money is rarely missed. This ensures that you will continue to make your chosen savings contributions month after month. The automatic approach also removes the temptation to spend investment money on other items before each monthly contribution is made.

OK, I UNDERSTAND THE CONCEPT OF PAYING MYSELF FIRST. BUT HOW MUCH SHOULD I BE PAYING MYSELF EACH MONTH?

There is no single answer to this question, only recommendations and various guidelines. We are each unique individuals. Ultimately, the answer to this question will differ for all of us. Some suggest that if you save 10% of your gross income, you'll have a comfortable retirement.

However, this depends on numerous factors, including:

- Age of the investor
- Projected years until retirement
- Amount of income over investor's lifetime
- Lifestyle expectations at retirement age
- Current liabilities (debt)
- Current assets (do you own your home, or owe a mortgage)
- Amount of return on your investments

Because of our uniqueness, we see that a simple answer of investing 10% of your gross income may not compute to your expectations. Service members' circumstances vary so widely, you'll need to determine what works for you as an individual.

It may be conceivable for a married couple to save 50% of their net income and still live a comfortable lifestyle. On the other hand, a new recruit just starting a career in the military may choose to start with 5%. At this point, no matter what amount you determine appropriate, it is just critical to begin today. Start developing the habits of saving and investing. Remember, these are lifelong skills you are developing and will be altered as your life changes. Your goal is to get rich slowly.

DEBT FREE? THE 50/30/20 BUDGET MAY WORK YOU

Many new recruits enter the military with a clean financial slate, meaning they have no debt or substantial financial obligations. It is likely that while completing basic training, the majority of recruits are exempt from common expenses the general public must face.

For example:

- Home mortgage
- Grocery bills
- Electric bills
- Gas bills
- Cable bills
- Credit card bills
- Automobile payments
- Auto insurance
- Home insurance
- Vehicle and home maintenance

Even after basic training, major expenses such as housing and meals are paid for by the military, leaving new recruits in good shape and virtually free of major expenses. And, as in Sergeant Major Austin's case, a great deal of the money that would have gone to all these traditional expenses could be routed directly into investments.

THE 50/30/20 BUDGET CONCEPT

You're in luck. The 50/30/20 budget is based on a concept that you previously studied; needs and wants. And, since new recruits are not obligated to so many common expenses, that makes this budget much more feasible.

- **50%—Must Haves**

    Fifty percent of your spending is designated for "must haves."

    Your goal is to limit your "must haves" to 50% of your after-tax income.

- **30%—Wants**

    Thirty percent of your spending is designated for "wants."

    Your "wants" are allowed to use 30% of your after-tax income.

- **20%—Savings**

    Twenty percent of your spending is designated for "Savings."

    The remaining 20% of your budget is automatically directed into your savings and investment plan.

Simplified, your target savings and investment goal is 20% of your net (after taxes) income. The 20% savings with this plan can be split in half; 10% simply placed into a regular savings account and the remaining 10% could be automatically directed into a conservative investment, such as the military's Thrift Savings Plan (TSP). When your regular savings reach a benchmark amount, invest all but $1,000 in a mutual fund or similar instrument and begin building it again. Simple plan? Yes. Effective? Absolutely.

TAKE ADVANTAGE OF AUTOMATIC DEDUCTIONS

Electronic deductions are an investor's best friend. After setting up automatic withdrawals for your investment funds, the money never enters your pocket and you won't have to worry about not spending it. You won't even miss it. You will have the peace of mind that your financial plan is now on autopilot.

ALREADY LIVING BELOW YOUR MEANS? YOU ARE THAT MUCH MORE PREPARED TO RETIRE.

Possibly the best part of saving 20% to 30% or more of your current income is that you are already budgeting to live below your means. The day you retire, the level of income you'll require will be less difficult to replace.

For example: if your salary is $45,000 the day of your retirement, and you have been saving 20% of your income, you would need to replace it with $36,000 from your retirement plan instead of the full $45,000. If you live on less than your income long enough, eventually it will become second nature.

NO TIME LIKE THE PRESENT

Having a difficult time deciding what is right for you? To begin, start small. You can always increase your designated savings and investment allotments later. If you're having difficulty deciding on what investments are best for you, try starting with just 1% of your net income. With time, if you determine the investment successful, increase the allotment to 2%, then try 5%. If you get a reenlistment bonus or raise in pay from earning a higher rank, half of it should be directed straight into your investment plan. Receive a gift or an inheritance? Place half of it in savings before you do anything else. And so on, and so forth.

As a brand-new military recruit, you may never have a better opportunity to begin securing your financial future.

A new recruit's advantages to create a prosperous financial plan may include:

- Steady income
- Limited financial obligations
- Benefits provided by the military promote the ability to save more cash
- Ability to take advantage of an investment plan at an extremely young age, allowing assets time to accrue

Most importantly, don't make excuses. Every one of us has things we'd rather spend our paycheck on. But if you're serious about being financially responsible, make saving and investing a priority. With a lifetime of growth, your early savings plan could potentially accelerate well beyond the average civilian's. The benefit of starting your plan today will maximize the compounding effects of your investments.

Chapter 22

Personal Finance Readjustment

"Numerous late fees were our financial wake-up call."

Master Sergeant Jacobson
US Air Force

My name is William Jacobson and I am a master sergeant in the US Air Force. In 2006, I returned from my first deployment to Iraq in support of Operation Iraqi Freedom. During my deployment, my wife, Theresa, and I had managed to save a great deal of my combat pay. But at the same time we accumulated a great deal of credit card debt. I know that sounds ridiculous. Why didn't we just pay cash rather than use credit cards for everyday goods and services? I was earning more money than ever, but we were still charging purchases on credit cards due to old habits and what we perceived as convenience.

Our wakeup call was a late payment for the third month in a row on one of our numerous credit cards. The late fee seemed unreasonably high. The only excuse we had was that we were disorganized and had no routine established to pay our bills on time. This initiated our decision to get a fresh start financially. To begin, we looked at what was important in our lives and decided to base our goals around what was most significant to us.

During a second deployment to Afghanistan, we were well aware that our savings plan would accelerate tremendously from the increased income from combat pay. Although we were anxious for me to be in harm's way, at the same time we were excited to pay off all of our credit card bills and our auto loan to finally become debt free. We also signed up for the military Savings Deposit Program (SDP). This is a wonderful, safe, convenient program that, at the time, earned 10% interest. By the completion of my second tour, we had accumulated a six-month emergency fund and organized a well-planned investment portfolio with the assistance of a responsible financial planner.

The following is a condensed version of the steps we followed to get our finances on the right track:

First:

We established a cash emergency fund. We started with $2,000.

SECOND:

We began to pay off the credit cards.

The high interest rates and potential late fees were completely working against us.

THIRD:

We moved out of married housing and became homeowners.

We loved the idea of building equity as home owners.

FOURTH:

We created a financial portfolio for our retirement.

This would include financial tools provided by the military, like the TSP, as well as other investments recommended by our financial planner, such as a Roth IRA.

It has been a little over five years since we had our wake-up call with the credit card bills. We actually had the thought that those ridiculous late fees were a blessing in disguise since they had convinced us to finally make our serious financial changes.

Chapter 23

Choosing a Financial Planner

INVESTING OVERVIEW

At this point, you have a grasp on the concept that investing your money is really a series of steps you must take. You've learned that it is a good idea to have the following in place before entering into an advanced financial plan:

- A comprehensive list of short- and long-term goals
- An established budget
- Elimination of all debt (except a mortgage)
- A fully funded emergency account (six months living expenses)
- A savings account
- A checking account

This is a solid foundation from which you can build wealth. After you have put these critical building blocks in place, you'll be able to advance your portfolio into a broader investment plan.

WHY USE A FINANCIAL PLANNER?

Assessing an individual company's value is a time-consuming process that requires exhaustive research of numerous facets and financial documentation from which to make an educated decision. But you're in luck—institutional investors called financial planners can do the work for you. Financial investment companies hire teams of professional investors to work together to analyze specific industries and companies. Together, these teams have the resources, experience, and expertise to grade a company's strengths and weaknesses.

A financial planner is a licensed professional, trained to assist investors by designing financial strategies that best fit their needs. They are educated in their field and have the ability to create a detailed plan. Your planner will help you devise specific goals. He or she will work closely with you to develop a plan tailored to your needs, based on your tolerance of risk and your chosen timeline.

To accomplish the tasks that financial planners do on your own would be an extraordinary feat, especially as a beginning investor. There will be fees involved if you use a professional financial planner. But the fees are minuscule compared to the money you could potentially lose and the time and resources required if you attempt this task on your own.

If you try to invest on your own, it is likely that you will learn the perils of the stock market by trial and error. More often than not, this method of learning results in the loss of the most precious commodity an investor has: time. The ability to accurately analyze an individual company's strength takes years of formal education and experience. When you are ready to begin investing, try using a qualified financial planner. The associated costs are well worth the return.

TYPICAL ERRORS MADE BY NOVICE INVESTORS

- Buying and selling stocks too frequently
- Buying and selling stocks based on media that presents misleading information or misinterpreted news stories
- Basing investments on emotions like fear and greed rather than facts and substantiated information
- Selling valuable stocks too early, resulting in missed profit opportunities
- Holding declining stocks too long

AT WHAT POINT SHOULD I SEEK A FINANCIAL PLANNER?

Once you have established your budget, created an emergency fund, eliminated the majority of your debt, and have specific goals in mind, you should begin seeking a competent financial planner. It is wise to wait until you have paid down your debt and funded an emergency account before investing. However, contacting a financial advisor sooner to help with decisions along the way is not a bad idea. An advisor's guidance may provide insight to accomplish your goals more efficiently. As long as you are accumulating cash in your savings account, you are saving money and earning interest, so don't feel obligated to make any hasty decisions.

CHOOSING A FINANCIAL PLANNER

Be sure to write down every question you have and interview several financial planners before making your selection. Advise the planner that you are just getting started with your investment plan and that you are interested in learning as much as you can along the way. If a planner is impatient or unwilling to answer your questions, request to work with a different planner or choose another company entirely. There are plenty available. Remember, your planner works for you, and he or she should value you and your time as a customer.

HOW DOES A FINANCIAL PLANNER GET PAID?

This is a question you should be very concerned with while deciding which financial institution is right for you. It may be in your best interest to hire a fee-only planner as opposed to one who earns a commission. Advisors who are paid a flat fee do not have an incentive to sell you products or services you may not need.

BENEFITS OF WORKING WITH A PROFESSIONAL

A professional financial planner can potentially:

- Increase your knowledge of the investment industry by answering any questions you may have about the process
- Provide insight during periods of market instability and notify you when an adjustment to your portfolio might be in order
- Utilize numerous resources to organize a strategy that will best meet your needs
- Advise you as to which investment opportunities are in your best interest
- Offer assistance in weighing risks and making decisions

THE FINAL DECISION

The bottom line: do not select a financial planner until he or she has disclosed a complete guideline of all fees, penalties, and commissions that may be charged. It is imperative that you have a full understanding of how the investment company you are using gets paid before you decide to take calculated risks in any investment.

It is easy to get over excited at this point and make hasty decisions. If you feel rushed when you are speaking with an investment company representative, explain that you need some time to think about your decision. While you are deciding, your money is safe in a savings account and isn't going anywhere. Use all the time you need to make investment decisions.

REQUIREMENTS FOR A SAVVY INVESTOR

Education
The more you are willing to learn regarding investments and investing strategies, the greater your ability will be to continually make sound decisions.

Patience
The lessons in this book focus on the importance of long-term financial planning and investing. Your financial plan will require time before it begins to turn a profit.

Foresight
Your ability to focus on the goals that will be important to you in the future, as well as the ones that are important to you now, will help you avoid impulsive spending and will be critical to your success.

Chapter 24

Day Trader

"I lost $35,000 in ten months."

Specialist Flannigan
US Army

WHAT IS DAY TRADING?

Day trading is the practice of buying and selling financial instruments within the same trading day. People engaged in day trading are not investors—they are traders. Day trading carries an extremely high risk and is more along the lines of gambling than investing. Tremendous losses are frequent, and novice investors are often warned against using day trading because of the fast-paced, high-energy, roller-coaster-ride effect it can produce. Day trading typically results in more massive losses and stomachaches than monetary gains. Day-trading schemes illustrate the opposite of what this book is attempting to emphasize. As an investor, your primary objective should be based on a long-term plan and not get-rich-quick schemes.

THE INEVITABLE DEMISE OF A DAY-TRADING SCHEME

I met Specialist Flannigan about a month after arriving at my first duty station while serving in the US Army. He also had just completed basic training and was assigned to my platoon. During some downtime on a field-training exercise, Specialist Flannigan had a chance to enlighten me on his familiarity with day trading during his short-lived college stint.

Like so many others, Specialist Flannigan had jumped into day trading with both feet. He had heard that this type of trading was more along the lines of gambling than investing. But the excitement and the promise of quick profits lured him in. He began day trading before learning how the markets worked, or even the basic definitions of investment terms and common financial tools.

Specialist Flannigan explained that as soon as he began day trading, his financial losses significantly outweighed any marginal gains. Eventually, he borrowed brokerage funds on margin and even used cash from his student loan to replenish his trading account. His dream of huge profits rapidly turned into a financial disaster. He continued trading until his initial capital was exhausted. Still convinced that he would eventually turn a profit, he ended his day-trading career by using money that covered his daily living expenses.

Ten short months after beginning his day-trading scheme, Specialist Flannigan had lost $35,000 and was completely broke. His grades were unacceptable, and the university had notified him that he was on academic probation. Without additional resources, he saw no alternative: he had to drop out of college.

Specialist Flannigan admitted that he truly understood what he had lost when he had to explain his predicament to his parents. Irreplaceable experiences in college had slipped away from him while he had been staring at a computer screen blindly chasing the latest stock moves.

Specialist Flannigan was very young when he began his day-trading scheme and was smart enough to learn from the results of his decisions. He has paid his debt in full from money he earned from a recent deployment and has now started a responsible budget and financial plan.

Let's take a look at how things could have gone for him if he hadn't blindly chased his dream of fast money.

If, at the age of twenty-five, he had invested his loss of $35,000.00 in a fund earning 4% interest, the account had the potential to grow to nearly $172,895.49 by the time he was sixty-five. If Flannigan had chosen to contribute another $300.00 per month, the account could possibly have grown to $527,483.89.

Although these figures would be lower if Specialist Flannigan had invested in a Roth IRA. However, he would have paid his taxes on the front end, leaving 100% of the remaining funds available to him after age fifty-nine-and-a-half.

Remember, varying interest rates, brokerage fees, and a volatile market can affect the outcome of investments, and these rough figures are for illustration purposes only.

THE TORTOISE VS. THE HARE

Remember that story? As the saying goes, a steady pace will certainly win the race when it comes to your investment plan. If you try shortcuts such as day trading, you are sure to learn this lesson the hard way. Your best bet is to let the professionals do the work for you and design your plan to get rich slowly.

Chapter 25

Deployment Finance

Since September 11, 2001, the potential for deployment while serving in the US military has increased significantly. For peace of mind, it is best to thoroughly prepare your financial plan ahead of time for the possible notification of going overseas. Then, if a deployment is announced, you can simply put your preorganized plan in motion. Preparing how you will handle your money before, during, and after each phase of a deployment is equally important and requires proper design.

Although a deployment certainly includes health and safety risks, the financial benefits can definitely be viewed in a positive light. Taking advantage of well-defined financial opportunities available during a deployment can result in financial security for you and your family. Why waste such a unique opportunity by frivolously spending the additional money on luxury items that have little or no long-term value? Cashing in on the additional income you receive while deployed can provide a hefty increase in your investment portfolio.

In this chapter, we will address financial issues in the following three phases of a deployment:

- Before deployment
- During deployment
- After deployment

BEFORE DEPLOYMENT

To state the obvious, preparing for a military deployment can be an extremely stressful event for service members and their families. The separation from family and other lifestyle changes at times can seem overwhelming.

One of the highest stressors prior to a deployment is organizing and maintaining your finances. Even while traveling halfway around the world, you must realize that you are still responsible for the financial obligations you leave behind. If you are unable to track your spending, you may accumulate an untold amount of financial debt, which will be waiting for you upon your return. By not preparing for all monetary commitments ahead of time, you may subject yourself to adverse consequences—such as bankruptcy.

However, constructing a solid financial plan well in advance will alleviate one of the leading causes of anxiety while deployed. Organizing your finances will give you a sense of empowerment, and a robust savings account will certainly provide something to look forward to when you get back home. You'll literally be turning the number one stressor into a positive goal.

    Because a deployment can drastically change your current financial plan, you must be prepared to reconstruct your plan to reflect the time frame that you will be away. For married couples, it is imperative that you design your new budget plan together. Struggling with finances is one of the most common problems military families experience during deployment. It is critical that couples work as a team while developing their financial plan. By getting organized well in advance, it should not be difficult to minimize confusion and avoid costly miscommunication.

SPECIFICS ABOUT PREPARING FOR DEPLOYMENT

On the next few pages, we'll take a detailed look at some important concepts when preparing for deployment. The information is not listed in any particular order. They are simply high points regarding preparation before a military deployment.

Adjust your current budget.

Prepare your finances to reflect the anticipated change in income and expenses for the designated time frame you'll be away. Begin by reviewing your current monthly household expenses and then adding or subtracting any differences for the time you expect to be away. The adjusted budget should give you a good idea of what financial issues you and your family will face each month while you are deployed. As a bonus, it may also reveal ways you can save money during deployment. The adjusted budget will provide critical information to whomever you designate to handle your finances until you return. By providing an accurate and detailed plan, you can rest assured that you have minimized the possibility of coming home to face any financial discrepancies.

For couples, try two checking accounts.

Financial difficulty is one of the most common problems military families experience during deployment. To eliminate miscommunication between spouses and avoid the possibility of overdrawing a shared checking account, many couples find it helpful to maintain two checking accounts. One is designated for monthly household expenses and the other is strictly for the deployed service member. This technique reduces the possibility of miscalculations as a result of two people half a world away from each other attempting to pay their expenditures from a single checking account.

Plan well in advance for a means to pay your bills on time.

You should make it a priority to find a means to meet all anticipated financial obligations throughout a deployment. Major expenses you may need to plan for could include credit cards, automobile loans, and mortgage or rent payments. Making arrangements well in advance is your personal responsibility to yourself and your family. Doing so will give you a sense of confidence and peace of mind, and you'll be more capable of focusing on your task at hand while serving in hazardous situations.

Use automatic bill pay.

Many monthly bills can now be paid automatically through an electronic process by your financial institution. This can be extremely convenient for you while you're on deployment. This process would especially apply to bills that typically do not fluctuate, such as automobile notes and mortgages. Contact your financial institution and ask to be advised of any available options.

Some of the high points of automatic bill pay to consider are:

- Easy to set up
- One less responsibility each month
- Payments will never be late
- Less worry about bills being paid
- Save money on stamps
- Payments will never be lost

Request electronic financial statements.

Prior to deployment, I requested that my financial provider send all monthly financial statements and notifications via e-mail. Doing so allowed me to stay up-to-date on all account information even while I was on the other side of the world. The system works so efficiently that I still use it today.

Some of the high points of requesting electronic financial statements to consider are:

- Receive information faster
- Eliminate lost paper documentation

- Address discrepancies before they escalate
- Eliminate surprises when returning home
- Spouses can receive and access identical information
- Information can be received as e-mail or by accessing your account online 24/7

Pay all bills on the same date.

By having all of your bills due on the same date, you can pay them all at once and not think about doing so again until next month. Setting this up can be as simple as contacting the billing department and requesting that the due date be changed to your preference. Some people prefer to have all bills due at the beginning of the month, and some prefer the middle. There is no right or wrong way. The concept simply promotes additional organization by enforcing a consistent routine every month.

Pay your bills via the Internet.

If you have not chosen to set up electronic auto bill pay, paying your bills online may be an option. Many businesses and utility companies encourage this practice. A few examples of bills to pay online may include utilities, mortgage, cell phone, and auto loans.

Request a trustworthy person to oversee your finances.

Although you may set up the majority of your financial transactions to be performed electronically, it is likely that you'll need someone to act on your behalf while you are away. After selecting a friend or family member to do so, present this person with a copy of your budget and any specific instructions for monthly requirements. Many situations will require the designee to provide proof that you've given this authority to him or her before a transaction can be completed.

Appoint a power of attorney.

Prior to deployment, it is important to appoint someone as your power of attorney. This is a legal instrument that deserves your serious consideration. Power of attorney is a designation that allows you to appoint someone to act in your place in financial or legal affairs. You'll need to be able to provide certified documentation proving you've given someone power of attorney.

When you grant a person power of attorney, you become the grantor, and the person with this power (your agent) is authorized, or granted, the power to act on your behalf in legal or business matters. Most often, service members choose to grant power of attorney to a spouse or other trusted family member. It is important for you to periodically review your existing power of attorney. Your changing needs may necessitate a revision, ensuring that your power of attorney accomplishes exactly what you need done and nothing else.

To establish a power of attorney, speak to your chain of command or your unit's legal department.

Consider using mini storage instead of maintaining an apartment.

For service members living in apartments, one possible option is to break the lease and put everything into storage. Losing your deposit to break the lease may be less expensive than paying rent for an empty apartment during the deployment. This also eliminates any monthly utility expenses and potential maintenance concerns or tragedies, like broken water pipes, fires, etc.

Make a plan to pay income taxes.

While away on deployment, service members are still responsible for paying taxes on time. If you are unable to plan the handling of your tax return before you are deployed, you must file for an extension with the IRS. Although the forms to do so can be found online, it is highly recommend that you speak with a representative of the IRS to be sure you take care of the matter properly. Decide in advance with your power of attorney how your income tax return will be filed and who will do it.

Consider a debit card vs. a credit card.

The difference between a credit card and a debit card is that a credit card company extends credit to you and you repay the money, with interest, for any purchases you make with the card. A debit card simply allows you to access funds directly from your checking or savings account. Since the debit card is not a line of credit, you don't pay interest on any of your purchases. Debit cards can be used as a form of payment throughout much of the world today, making them very convenient while deployed.

Establish a will and life insurance.

As you are well aware, military deployments involve certain degrees of risk. The military, as well as private corporations offer life insurance plans. A will is a legal document that instructs others how you want your property distributed after your death. If you have any questions regarding either, speak to your chain of command to be directed to a professional who can ensure that you are making informed decisions. If you need further assistance, you can also visit your base's legal office.

Consider getting traumatic injury insurance.

Prior to deployment, it may be in your best interest to determine if you qualify for traumatic injury insurance. This type of protection may be offered by the Service Members' Group Life Insurance (SGLI) program.

REVIEW OF PRE-DEPLOYMENT FINANCIAL TIPS

Additional financial preparation and planning information can be provided by those within your chain of command's finance department. Here are some finer points that may assist you while working out your own plan:

- Select a family member you trust to be given power of attorney, and file any appropriate paperwork.
- Set up automatic bill payment whenever possible.
- Select a family member you trust to take care of your bills. This person may be the same one who holds power of attorney.
- Notify your current financial institutions and creditors of your deployment and provide them with contact information for your power of attorney.

- Provide pertinent account numbers, user names, or passwords if necessary with your power of attorney.
- Design a system to save all receipts as well as legal and financial documentation. This could be as simple as making a folder for each of these categories.
- Review your life insurance policies with your providers and beneficiaries.
- If at all possible, be sure that you have an emergency savings account with six months living expenses.
- Take advantage of the Savings Deposit Program (SDP) while you are serving in a combat zone.
- Research a traumatic injury protection policy. Such policies are designated to help your family if you suffer from a traumatic injury.
- Complete a will and appoint a personal representative.

PREDEPLOYMENT CHECKLISTS

Financial

- Have you adjusted your current budget to reflect your new income and expenses?
- If you are married, have you discussed the plan thoroughly with your spouse?
- Have you designated someone to pay the bills?
- Does your budget consider the following:
    ◇ Utilities
    ◇ Rent/mortgage

- ◇ Food
- ◇ Automobile maintenance
- ◇ Insurance
- ◇ Loan payments
- ◇ Emergencies
- ◇ Babysitting
- ◇ Presents
- ◇ Savings
- ◇ Long-distance phone calls
- ◇ Postage
- ◇ Travel (leave)
- ◇ Entertainment

- If you are married, have you established two checking accounts?
- Do you have a plan for paying income taxes?

Legal

- Is your spouse's emergency contact information on record and current?
- Have you established a plan for moving your household goods?
- Do you know your spouse's Social Security number?
- Have you designated a power of attorney?
- Does your spouse have a government identification card?
- Are your wills established and current?

Documentation

- Have you reviewed the following documents to make sure they are current, and are they secured in a safety-deposit box?
    - ◇ Power of attorney Birth certificates Wills
    - ◇ Citizenship documentation Savings bonds Naturalization papers Charge account numbers
    - ◇ Inventory of household goods
    - ◇ Real estate (deeds, titles, mortgages, leases) Family Social Security numbers
    - ◇ Car titles
    - ◇ Bank account numbers Insurance policies Marriage certificate

DURING DEPLOYMENT

Deployment financial tips The following are some tips to consider while on a deployment:

SAVE YOUR HARD-EARNED DEPLOYMENT CASH.

From a monetary standpoint, a deployment can be the opportunity of a lifetime. In fact, deployment pay can be an enormous financial boost. Deployment money has the potential to catapult your savings account balance well beyond your expectations. Make sure you put an investment strategy into effect before you leave, and watch your savings increase by leaps and bounds.

WATCH OUT FOR TEMPTATIONS WHILE AWAY FROM HOME.

Long deployments can increase the temptation to give in to major impulse purchases. Some bases even offer service members the opportunity to order new customized vehicles or motorcycles directly from the PX. Just remember to ask yourself, were these luxury items included in my financial plan?

GET AWAY FROM THE "I MAY NOT LIVE TO SEE TOMORROW" PHILOSOPHY.

"I might as well spend it today—I might not live to see tomorrow." We had a few soldiers in our company blow their hard-earned pay based on this philosophy before and during our deployment. Guess what? They returned home broke and were right back where they started, with little to show for their sixteen months in combat. Others who did not handle their finances with this attitude were in much better shape upon their return. Try establishing loftier goals, like purchasing a new home when you return, attending college, or attaining the peace of mind that you have a tremendous jump start on your retirement.

BE CAUTIOUS ABOUT BORROWING MONEY DURING DEPLOYMENT.

Be conservative and careful when considering taking on a loan during deployment. Base your monthly income on your post deployment paycheck, not your deployment income.

AFTER DEPLOYMENT

With deployments spanning twelve months or more, many service members will see their savings accounts increase dramatically. However, upon your return, you must adjust your spending to reflect your current pay rate at that time. Remind yourself that your monthly income could be reduced by half.

Veterans returning from deployment often purchase large-scale items as a reward for their hard work overseas. Examples could be a new vehicle, boat, ATV, snowmobile, or an extravagant wedding ceremony. Let's examine the purchase of a brand-new SUV in comparison to placing the same money in a moderate-risk mutual fund for the next fifty years.

	Funds Spent	Interest Earned	Today's Value	Value in 5 Years	Value in 50 Years
SUV	$40,000	0%	$40,000	$10,000	$0
Mutual Fund	$40,000	4%	$40,000	$48,667	$284,267

To summarize, when a deployment is announced, financial opportunities may be your last concern. But ignoring money matters at this stressful time could be a costly mistake. The better you prepare today, the better you'll be able to protect your family and your finances while you are away. For more information, schedule an appointment to meet with your unit's finance department. They will be able to provide additional assistance regarding your unique personal finance issues and specific information pertaining to your unit's anticipated deployment.

CHAPTER 26

MONEY SAVING TIPS

"We pay cash for everything we purchase."
Staff Sergeant Anderson
US Air Force

US Air Force Staff Sergeant Anderson admitted that he had his wife to thank if any money was saved in his household. Before becoming engaged to his fiancé, Staff Sergeant Anderson made many of the typical impulse purchases many young people make when they first begin receiving a paycheck. His first major investment after his enlistment was a brand new truck, as well as a brand new all-terrain vehicle shortly after. In order to get the vehicles, he financed almost the entire cost of both. After paying his monthly obligations to the lenders and insurance, his checking account often-times fell below the minimum amount and was charged an additional fee.

After their marriage, Mr. and Mrs. Anderson realized that if they did not make serious changes to their spending habits, they would be in debt for years to come. Together, they decided to set distinct goals. To expedite the process, they sold Mrs. Anderson's vehicle for cash, which she fully owned. They used the cash from the sale to pay down debt. Then they reestablished their budget to pay off the other vehicle and two major credit cards over the next two years. After making the necessary sacrifices to accomplish their mission, they also decided they would never pay anything but cash for all expenditures, including vehicles.

Finding the right techniques to save money is a challenge for all of us. While the idea of setting aside a portion of your income for your investment plan is appealing, many people find it difficult to actually do so. Trial and error may be the best way to find what works for you. The following are some of the Andersons' money-saving tips that worked for them:

GENERAL METHODS TO SAVE MONEY:

- Bring lunches, snacks, and beverages to work with you.
- Make coffee at home rather than visiting the local coffee shop.
- Rent movies to watch at home rather than going to the theater.
- Quit smoking. (This will improve your health, too!)
- Pay with cash, not credit.

- Buy used. You can do this by checking classified ads in your local paper, looking online, shopping at used-retail shops, and going to garage sales.
- Read more books. This hobby is free if you use the library, and you can learn something as well!
- Assess the importance of any collections you have.

  You may be willing and able to give up a collection or two to save money, or even sell off a collection you've lost interest in.
- Agree to limit gift giving. Limit the amount you spend for birthdays, or draw names for the holidays.
- Give yourself a haircut. The military haircut is the easiest one to give yourself.
- For homeowners, seal your home to prevent drafts.

  This will save a great deal on heating and cooling costs.

VEHICLES

- Never buy new. Shop online for quality preowned vehicles.
- If your old car still works reliably, keep driving it.
- Pay cash for your vehicles.
- Properly inflate your tires. It will decrease fuel consumption.
- Slow down when driving. This also will decrease fuel consumption.
- Maintain your automobile. This will save on repairs as well as decrease fuel consumption.

BANKING

- Use electronic bill pay. Enrolling in automatic bill pay can reduce rates and fees, and you save money on postage and checks. It's good for the environment, too.
- Pay with cash. Issue yourself an allotment of cash to use rather than using debit cards or ATM cards, which may charge fees. Also, it is too easy to spend money with credit and debit cards; you won't think about your purchases as thoroughly.
- Avoid banks with excessive fees. Shop around for accounts with low or no fees.

CREDIT CARDS

- Cancel them. You'll save by purchasing fewer items and not paying interest.
- If you must have one, ask for a rate reduction. If you reliably pay your bill on time and threaten to drop the card if you can't have a lower interest rate, companies may agree to the reduction.
- Never carry your credit card in your wallet. You will have to think about the purchase before you use it.
- Consolidate your credit card debt. This can lower your interest rate and the time it will take to pay off your debt.

FOOD

- Make a shopping list and stick to it. It will help keep you from making unplanned and unnecessary purchases.
- Frequently eat at the chow hall. Use the PX's grocery store flyer. Plan meals based on the items that are on sale.
- Use coupons, especially on sale items to save even more.
- Never grocery shop when you are hungry. You'll buy more.
- Stock up on staple items when they are on sale.
- Pack a cooler on long drives or day trips. It saves money compared to eating out.
- Try cooking with a slow cooker. Slow cooker meals often combine readily available and low-cost foods.
- Freeze baked dishes. Make casseroles when ingredients are on sale and freeze them for when you don't have time to cook. You will save twice, by purchasing sale items and by eliminating the need to eat out.
- Cook with generic products. The quality of generics and store brands is often identical to name brands while the price is much more affordable.

LET US REVIEW GETTING OUT OF DEBT

- Build up an emergency fund first, and pay off debt afterward.

- Stop using credit cards to make it to the next paycheck, and enjoy cutting them up.
- Don't overpay your debts. Follow your budget so you have enough for routine expenses.
- Be patient.
- Use the snowball method to organize your debt elimination.
- First, to get your momentum going, attack the smallest balance of debt with all the extra cash available; then, move on to the next lowest balance of debt.
- However, it may be in your best interest to pay off sources of debt with the highest interest first.
- Set realistic goals.
- If you began accumulating debt four or five years ago, recognize that it may take you more than this amount of time to eliminate your debt.
- Stop spending!
- Recognize eliminating your accumulated debt will be a long and slow process.
- You may not see immediate results with your new plan, but you must realize that in time you will succeed.
- Stop borrowing money. Period.
- Completely eliminate the use of credit cards, car loans, cash advances, home equity loans, etc. If you can't afford to make a purchase with cash, you cannot afford it!

- Plan ahead of time to commit anticipated bonuses and pay raises to eliminating debt, or put these in your long-term savings plan.
- For motivation, track your debt reduction on a spreadsheet.
- The data will indicate the effectiveness of your plan as well as provide a time frame for getting completely out of debt.

LET US REVIEW WAYS TO AVOID DEBT

- Simply don't use credit for anything.
- Use cash for all your purchases and don't take on any debt, with the only exception being the purchase of a home.
- Save up the money and purchase with cash.
- By the time you've saved up the money, you may determine that you don't even need the item anymore.
- Make a plan.
- Any plan is better than no plan at all.
- Create a budget.
- A structured budget is the key to avoiding overspending and unaccountable use of credit.
- Every month, set your budget to spend less than you earn.
- Cut up your credit cards.

- If you must have a credit card, set the limit low and keep the card at home.
- Contribute the maximum amount to your 401(k).
- Each time your cost-of-living allowance (COLA) increases or you get promoted in rank, increase your 401(k) contribution by 1% to 2%. If you don't ever see the money, how can you miss it?
- Cook your own meals.
- Avoid eating out, except on very special occasions.
- Visit friends and be creative on how to entertain yourself and your family. Soon you'll discover ways to do this without spending a penny.
- Be aware of upcoming expenses and plan for them accordingly, so you don't have to use any type of credit when they are due.
- Have open communication with your spouse regarding your finances to avoid competing interests.
- Start a garden. Some military bases have community gardens.
- With a small plot of ground, you can grow tomatoes, peas, beans, and even herbs. No garden? No problem. You can grow a ton of vegetables in containers right on your back porch. Gardening is inexpensive, healthy, and fun!
- Observe spending tendencies and place limits on them.

- Develop good habits early on to set an example for your children.
- Keep an open mind while trying to find the tools that work for you.
- If the tools aren't working, keep searching to discover new tools.
- You can find countless personal budgeting ideas on the Internet.
- Put a note in your wallet stating the following: "Is this a need or a want?"
- Focus on paying yourself first.
- Be aware that the only person you are in control of is yourself.
- If your spouse is partly the cause of your financial debt, try leading by example when you begin changing your spending habits.
- When your savings account begins to reflect your efforts at the end of each month, your spouse may be excited to follow your example.
- Be willing to make sacrifices.
- Routinely examine your needs versus your wants.
- For inspiration, subtract the cost of "wants" from your monthly budget and multiply the amount by twelve. The annual summation of "wants" will expose the amount of money you will have in your savings account at the end of the year. This simple exercise

is what convinces many to feel differently about the expense of the "wants" in question.
- Plan your budget using an electronic spreadsheet or program.
- By tracking your expenses electronically, you will be able to see at a glance how much you spent in each category so you can easily spot your problem areas.
- Envision your future.
- Stay focused on where you will be five, ten, or fifteen years from now. It will be here sooner than you think.
- Routinely educate others in your unit so that they too can choose to avoid costly financial pitfalls throughout their own careers.

Chapter 27

A Final Success Story

"I have benefited from many of the unique opportunities the military has to offer."
Lieutenant Junior Grade Wilkins
US Navy

Coming out of Officer Candidate School (OCS) in 2008, I was in better shape than many of my classmates. First, I was fortunate enough to qualify for the Health Professions Loan Repayment Program (HPLRP), which paid off approximately $75,000 of student loans over my initial three-year Navy commitment. I would also be commissioned as a lieutenant junior grade, increasing my earning potential. Second, I purchased most of my uniform items from a Navy Marine Corps thrift store. Many of my classmates ended up with new credit cards that they had to charge over $1,000 in uniform costs their first day in the Navy. Additionally, I entered the Navy with no credit card debt and an old car (1989!) that had been given to me by a family member. Essentially, all of my net income was disposable income.

My first year in the Navy, I saved nothing. I never had any personal financial training and didn't know how to even begin saving.

At the end of my first year in the Navy (at twenty-five years old), I was selected to deploy to Afghanistan for six months. During downtime, I began reading blogs on personal finance and reflected on my financial goals for the future. I switched banks from a credit union with unwieldy debit card restrictions to a bank where I could manage all of my checking, savings, retirement, and insurance accounts. I opened up a Roth IRA and set up automatic deductions each paycheck to reach $5,000 per year maximum. I also enrolled in TSP—directing 25% of my take-home pay to the fund.

With tax-exempt pay and bonuses, I knew this would be an opportunity to fast track my financial goals. I designated 100% of my special pay and bonuses to be automatically deposited into my TSP. (TSP limits are higher when deployed.) I also set up two additional savings accounts—one for my emergency fund (goal: $10,000) and one for my "slush fund" (goal: $5,000) to be used for travel and various presents (birthday, wedding, Christmas, etc.). I not only met all of my financial goals but opened another savings account—mortgage savings—and was able to fund that with approximately $5,000.

While I have learned a lot about personal finance the last few years and benefited from many of the unique opportunities the military has to offer, I would recommend the following to anyone in the military:

1. Check to see if you qualify for any student loan reimbursement programs when you join the military (and apply every year). Consider placing your student loans in military deferment.
2. Take ten minutes every month to review your Leave and Earnings Statement (LES) line by line. By doing this, I discovered that I was incorrectly listed as a resident of Hawaii (which has state taxes) when I am actually a resident of Washington State (which does not have state taxes). Additionally, I realized I had been charged taxes on my tax-exempt leave days post deployment.
3. Find military mentors you respect—either senior enlisted or officers—and ask them about their financial experiences, tips, and advice.
4. Read as many personal finance blogs and books as you can and find a method or author that you can relate to. Find a banking institution that you trust and that fits with your financial goals.

Chapter 28

Summary

WHICH GROUP WILL YOU BE IN?

If you look back at the information in this book five, ten, even fifty years from now, will you be in debt, with no savings plan, and wondering what you were thinking when you didn't take advantage of this knowledge? Or will you be confident with your finances and proud of yourself for securing your own financial future?

JUST REMEMBER THESE FIVE FUNDAMENTALS TO GET YOURSELF STARTED:

1. Follow your written budget to assure a lifestyle within your means.
2. Establish a short-term emergency fund ($2,000).
3. Pay off your debts—including your vehicle, excluding your mortgage.

4. Establish a long-term emergency fund (six months' salary).
5. Routinely interact with your financial planner and invest 15% to 25% (or more) of your income.
6. Use any excess funds to pay off your home mortgage early (reenlistment bonuses, tax returns…).

That's it. Six basic steps. By starting out with these six basic steps, the finer points will definitely fall into place.

EDUCATE YOUR FELLOW SERVICE MEMBERS

Many new recruits have just finished high school, and the military may be their first steady, paying job. It is highly possible these young service members have not yet learned how to set a budget or financially plan for their future. Without financial guidance, they may slip through the cracks and find themselves losing the most precious commodity when it comes to investing—time.

You have learned a lot about how you are in control of your financial future. I hope that you'll share this information with as many service members as possible. I felt a tremendous sense of satisfaction when I was able to teach new recruits the financial basics, especially before they learned of life's financial pitfalls through trial and error.

With annual revisions and contributions from readers like you, it is my personal goal to perfect the presentation of *Military Millionaires* so that they may pass on these valuable lessons to their fellow service members.

I sincerely thank each service member in every branch of the United States military. Your selfless service and devotion to protecting our great nation and the beliefs on which it was founded is an honor you will proudly carry throughout your lifetime.

Good luck to you with your military career and your financial prosperity!

Sincerely,
Michael S. Hamlin
Veteran and Author

> Do you have a financial story you would like to share with your fellow service members?
> Visit www.military-millionaires.com to learn how.

About the Author

Michael Stephen Hamlin received his bachelor of administration degree in finance from Western Michigan University and worked five years in the insurance industry before volunteering for service in the US Army. Sgt. Hamlin served four years including a 16-month tour in Iraq as an infantry team leader. During his service, Sgt. Hamlin observed many young and older military personnel making both good and bad financial decisions. He hopes this book will enhance good financial decisions, and aid many service members in taking control of their finances and building their wealth.